CELIA GREEN

The Corpse and the Kingdom

CELIA GREEN

The Corpse and the Kingdom

oxford-forum.org

© 2023 Celia Green

ISBN: 978-1-9160906-82

Contents

Aphorisms

The concept of a good social structure is a contradiction in terms. A good escape committee in a prison camp is recognised by the speed with which it renders itself unnecessary.

* * *

I am not concerned that society should try to do me good; I should only like it to try to do me less harm.

* * *

People are always waiting for other people to endorse them. They never reach the point where they are endorsed enough (in fact society is scarcely willing to endorse people at all), so they never have enough self-confidence to start being generous.

* * *

The only way to avoid risking disappointment in life is to ensure it. People are very keen on doing this on behalf of the young.

* * *

Great progress has been made since the human race naively imagined that its home planet was the centre of the universe. Now we know that it isn't, but that *it doesn't matter. We needn't notice.*

* * *

Every human being must desire either to exalt himself or to degrade everyone else.

* * *

The true object of aggression is the unknowability of existence.

* * *

People profess to think fame uninteresting. This argues a contempt for the opinions of the human race which may be justified but is not consistent; if the opinions of the human race over several lifetimes are of little account, what valuation can be set on the contents of a single lifetime?

* * *

One should have objective relationships, not human ones.

* * *

If you know your own mind, only lack of money stands between you and felicity. Of course if you don't, which is much more common, money may not help you too much.

* * *

Social psychology

You should be on the lookout for the feeling of someone peering lovingly at your frustrations from behind a carefully arranged facial expression and soft words. The soft words, you should carefully note, do you no good at all.

* * *

The human race is fairly keen on expressions of 'goodwill'. They like to 'congratulate' people. These 'congratulations' and expressions of 'goodwill' are supposed to prove that they are benevolent.

* * *

The human race has no time to live like vegetables and, dimly, knows it.

* * *

They seek in peace the intensity of war. So long as intensity is not understood, how can the world have peace?

* * *

The human race has some dim knowledge of the liberation that comes sometimes in extremity; of battle-ecstasy.

* * *

'La raison du plus fort est toujours la meilleure' is as true today as ever it was. Only now 'le plus fort' is always the agent of the collective.

* * *

An interesting belief of sane persons is that it is *difficult* even to realise that other people are there. It is supposed to take a young child quite a long time to contrive a way of thinking of itself as separate from its environment. This is all in line with the value placed on 'maturation' and verbal thought. Obviously a very young child does not know any language well enough to think verbally, and so it is held to be exceedingly half-witted. (Incidentally, Einstein did most of his thinking non-verbally.)

* * *

Opinions

The human race not only likes discussing opinions, but desires all opinions to be as crude as possible. If one asks oneself why this should be, one can only suppose that it is part of their general policy of cultivating feeblemindedness to an extent that could not have been supposed possible.

Alternatively, one might suppose that, should they succeed in teaching some more chimpanzees sign language, they would want the whole of human culture to be accessible to chimpanzees, and do not wish to hold any opinions which might be a trifle complex.

* * *

The following fragments have been found in Wittgenstein's wastepaper basket (*Papierkorb*):

What does a person mean when he says he is motivated to do something? What is a motive? Have you ever seen one?

What can anyone mean by saying that they have had experiences they cannot exactly describe? What are you unable to describe? Tell me.

When I see a man walking across the road, and think, 'perhaps that man is an automaton' – what is the result of that? I get a strange feeling.

It is important to realise that there is nothing other than the language game. If there were anything else, what could we say about it?

What people call thinking is an illness; it is what happens when the language game gets disordered. Philosophy should lay down rules for the language game so that it never gets disordered; then philosophy can stop.

* * *

Patronage

In the ideal socialist world it would be illegal for financial support to be obtained except from such entities as the Nuffield Foundation. As it is, it is not actually illegal for individuals to support individuals, it is just opposed by a very strong taboo, which is strictly obeyed nearly all of the time.

* * *

Let us, for the sake of argument, suppose that life is in fact a dream. Now the characteristic of a dream is that it is related to a state known as 'waking life' in this way: that when a person is awake, everything that went on in the state of 'dreaming' seems to him trivial.

APHORISMS

I: THE ANTECEDENTS OF SOCIETY

1

The social contract – I

The power of society depends on the power of the lie. The power of the lie is very great.

The power of the individual depends on the right of possession and the sanctity of facts. Neither of these is recognised by society. It is only under capitalism that there is a recognition of the individual's right to the facts. He has a right to the facts about his possessions. Consequently facts are themselves regarded as possessing a certain value. In a socialist society no one has any right to the facts. There is no point in facts at all. The power of the state, which is the sole good, is best safeguarded by there being no facts.

People are subjective, but some people are more subjective than others and those who believe in society are the most subjective of all. This is because they have abandoned to society their right to assess facts for themselves, in return for the power that society will give them over others. The high priests of society are social workers, doctors and psychiatrists. Their function is to convince others that they are being subjective if they venture to criticise society.

2

Two introductory scenarios

First introductory scenario

You are perceiving things, but the status of your perceptions is entirely indeterminate. You do not know the significance of this situation, or whether it has any. Among the things that you seem to perceive are other people, but you are unable to determine whether they have consciousness, as you seem to yourself to have. Perhaps they are automata. Or perhaps they are just hallucinatory figures in your hallucinatory dream.

Second introductory scenario

What you are perceiving seems to be a physical universe and it seems to be possible to infer certain things about the past history of this universe. It is possible to suppose that your consciousness is a by-product of physical and chemical events in your organism, and that other people are conscious in a similar way to yourself as a result of similar events in their organisms.

The human race, of which you are a part, seems to have been on the planet on which you are living for a very small part of the inferable history of the physical universe. The lifetime of the human race, and the space it occupies, is infinitesimal even in relation to the time and space that the human race is able to infer in the physical universe that surrounds it. It is inferred that there may be millions of other stars as well able to possess life-bearing planets as our sun. It is inferred that previous life forms on this planet, such as the dinosaurs, occupied it for tens of millions of years.

The human race has a strong tendency to believe that what the human race regards as good and valuable is of great importance. What is important to a human being (and in what other sense could the word important have meaning) is to be determined by reference to the local consensus of belief about what is important in the social environment which surrounds that human being.

3

Two preliminary scenarios

Preliminary scenario 1

Each individual finds himself involved in a strange and complicated story. He cannot remember exactly how it began. If he believes what the other people in the story tell him, he is going to die, which means perhaps that he will cease being conscious of anything again. The environment in which he finds himself is one of staggering complexity. The universe of astronomy surrounds his planet, leading to no edge, but to abysses of unimaginable mathematical paradox. The earth under his feet is supposedly made of particles, the study of which leads to no final definition of their ultimate types and characteristics, but to abysses of unimaginable mathematical paradox. Probably there is in his home a box with a flat front which shows moving coloured pictures of his world, impressing upon him the intolerable multifariousness of all the forms of life that have ever crawled or swum or flown in the darkest and deepest, hottest and coldest, wettest and driest crevices of his planet. Again, no precise limit can be set upon their numbers, though vague estimates can be made of the number of unclassified insects of a certain type that probably remain to be found and labelled in the basin of the Amazon.

There seem to be other people in this story with him, but there is a great difference between himself and them. He is conscious of his own feelings, but only by implication and inference of theirs. Are they conscious of themselves as he is conscious of himself? If he talks to them about this they usually discourage him from thinking about such an absurd question (but he may have read about dreams in which figures in the dream argue vigorously and mockingly with the dreamer about whether they are real). Is his the only consciousness? What is the point of all this, and does the point of it have anything at all to do with him? Is the whole universe a casual uncaused appearance, a sudden shocking bauble emerging from unbeing?

Why should it? Why should it not? What could cause such a thing? Of course his ideas of caused and uncaused break down; as usual, at the edge of things his thought is mocked by the unimaginable.

Perhaps the universe is just a material thing and his consciousness only an accidental by-product. That is to say the universe is nothing but this turbulence of forces, ultimately based upon unimaginable mathematical relationships. The turbulence has happened to produce living forms, that is patterns of matter that are able to generate further similar patterns, and those which are of some complexity seem to themselves to be conscious. But the semblance of consciousness has no more reality than the electromagnetic field of a machine; it will stop being there when the machine stops, and the mechanical mathematical universe will go on indifferently.

Is all this his dream and will he ever awaken? Are all the people and perhaps the animals dreaming too, and is this a communal hallucination in which they are all caught? Or is he the dream, as some have suggested, of a magician or a god? If so, what are the intentions of the dreamer?

Preliminary scenario 2

Supposing that the physical world may be taken at face value and that the inferences drawn from it about the past of the planet are correct, we have the following picture of the past of the human race. Through geological ages the world cooled and life began to swarm upon it. Life forms struggled for survival and more complex forms emerged and developed. Very, very recently in geological time, tribes of ape-men began to appear approximating to present-day humans in intelligence. Tribal groups wandered and fought for territory. Gradually they began to settle in favourable places and to develop some of the techniques that were possible to settled dwellers, always subject to attack by other marauding tribes who envied their advantages. But settlement became gradually the predominant style of life, and settled tribes began to manage their affairs so that they remained in one place for long periods of time. There was little freedom for individuals within these tribes, which began to be what we call civilisations, and increased control of the environment was gained slowly. It could have been gained much faster if the human race had had a tendency to value the sort of ability among its members that might lead to advances in knowledge, but it did not. Similarly, species might have evolved much more rapidly if they had had a tendency to recognise and protect those individuals among their number who differed most extremely from the norm in a way that would tend towards the next evolutionary development; but why should they do that? Why should it seem of any importance to lungfish, even supposing them to have a high level of intelligence, that they should evolve sooner rather than later into amphibians that could live on the land? If it had seemed of importance to them, they could have protected and aided the fish with the largest lungs and the strongest forefins.

The advantages that might have accrued to the human race from a tendency to value and protect intellectually gifted individuals were less remote, but still unquantifiable, and it would have been necessary to appreciate intellectual ability for its own sake, not for the benefits it might produce, which would have been difficult to foresee. Nevertheless, it is possible to imagine that it might have happened. A tribe which happened to have it inbuilt into its genetic constitution that it admired and protected exceptional individuals among its members might have been at a sufficient advantage in the struggle for survival for this genetic constitution to have become predominant. There is little sign that this happened; perhaps the timescale within which the human race was struggling towards settled civilisation was simply too short for such a factor to take precedence over the survival value which attached to other factors, such as the value for the tribe of compliant members, and the value for individual survival of destructive jealousy towards individual rivals.

However, even so, the advances in control of the environment built up exponentially, slow as they were. The human race farmed better, made better tools, built better shelters to live in. But the great leap in control came suddenly and accidentally, as a result of a short period of increased freedom for individuals. This came about as a result of the development of the idea of individual property and commerce. This made it possible for some individuals to gain a good deal of freedom for themselves within the tribal framework, and the ability to make use of the commercial possibilities was correlated with intellectual power. The concept of individual property was associated with the right of the individual to bequeath property (i.e. freedom) on his death; he tended to leave it to his descendants, and they tended to inherit the abilities which had made it possible for him to gain his property in the first place. Only 'tended' of course, but that is all one can hope for in an evolutionary situation. This made possible an enormous expansion in scientific knowledge and a development of idealistic principles, which included, at least for a time, an ideal of appreciation of exceptional individuals and of progress as an abstract concept.

But the tribal forces in human psychology reasserted themselves. So much had been gained in the way of knowledge, now they could see their way (or thought they could) towards living perfectly adequate tribal lives without allowing individuals any further freedom from tribal control. People could live blandly and uneventfully, they could enjoy the pleasures of feeding and breeding, they could be free from disease and discomfort until they blandly and uneventfully died. There was no longer any need for intellectuals. The tribe would have a few in the tribal universities but no one would have to be allowed to become rich any more. The tribe would take possession of all the advantages created by individual freedom and use them to keep individuals in a state of contented unfreedom.

This is the point of history at which we live.

4

The social contract – II

In the views of exponents of how society came to be constituted as it is (or was at the time, or should be), we note fairly constantly a willingness to ascribe untrammelled and overriding power to the legislators of the community, together with infallibility. In early accounts some justification for society's claim to possession of the individual is felt to be necessary. This is provided either by God, who bestows upon kings their divine right, or by a social contract, which is mythical, even if some writers lose sight of its historical implausibility. Desiring the advantages of an organised community, it is supposed that individuals freely choose to obey the government that shall be chosen by majority preference; hence minorities have nothing to complain of, as they have entered the situation of their own free will. So conflict is avoided.

I would have formulated the situation myself by supposing that, at a sufficiently primitive stage, when there was some realistic possibility of a dissident or disadvantaged individual choosing to fend for himself, there was a real balance of advantages and disadvantages for each individual which led, on the whole, to his preferring to remain, in fairly unstable equilibrium, in the settlement or compound occupied by his group. Fairly disharmonious associations of this kind gradually evolved social structures which reduced the squabbling and maximised the stability of the enterprise. At the time of, say, Hobbes, there was relatively little opportunity for any individual to dissociate himself from the pressures and demands of his society. By now there is even less.

We note that writers on political theory wish conflict between the individual and society to be an impossibility, or if not impossible, at least a clear aberration from a perfect underlying harmony.

5

Frustration by society

Frustration by society – I

It is the fundamental purpose of society to frustrate the individual in any attempt to react appropriately to the awareness of the existential predicament.

For this reason, it is not permitted to consider the idea of individuals being frustrated by society.

It is remarkable to see how young people, who are not seemingly of particularly exalted intelligence, produce the correct social responses when meeting someone who claims to be in a position of frustration. They immediately start to insist, explicitly or implicitly, that the small struggles which the frustrated one is able to make constitute a large and ample opportunity. 'But surely, you *are* doing research?' they say, wrinkling the brow. 'Surely this *is* research?'

A person who is frustrated by society may well imply, or even say in so many words, that he has about as much chance of enlisting social support for his plans by rational exposition as he would have of enlisting the enthusiastic agreement of a committee of mentally deranged chimpanzees by the same means. The response to such implications is always for the socially-adjusted one to imply in return that society is not a committee of mentally deranged chimpanzees, but an open-minded, omniscient, benevolent and totally impartial deity, which will naturally respond in a fair and openhanded manner to any proof of merit on the part of the small individual cowering before it.

Consequently, all effort should be devoted to 'proving one's merits' to this deity.

An understanding of this exchange of implication and counter-implication is sufficient to render a good deal of human conversation very dull.

For example, 'All I can do is to wish you every success with your new book,' means, 'In spite of all you have said about the unlikelihood of your book making a million pounds, which is what you say you need to do some research that means something, writing books is a socially approved means of proving your merits to society, and if you are really meritorious, society will support you in your plans, and if it does not, you should not be supported in your plans because you are not really meritorious.'

Does this expression of 'goodwill' make the recipient feel in the slightest respect invigorated or liberated? Exactly the contrary, of course. He is reminded that almost everyone sees things exactly like the person he is speaking to. He is reminded that, whatever he can do, it will never be taken as any indication that he is in a position of frustration.

Beware of the human race and their expressions of 'goodwill'. Such things can be, in their covert way, not good for one's health.

Frustration by society – II

One of the strongest taboos is that on the concept of being frustrated by society. It is, according to this taboo, absolutely impossible for anyone to be suffering because they are given no chance to use their abilities.

One may ask oneself: what exactly would people like one to feel? They do not seem to be exactly keen on one expressing one's state of frustration. They always talk as if they expect one to be identified with the tiny scale of operation which is possible to one.

I think it is clear that what they mostly wish one to feel is humiliation. You are supposed to feel that not being given a chance to do things corresponds to a judgment which has been passed upon you. That it is right, that you are the sort of person who deserves no better, than to live in a straitjacket.

You are supposed to identify yourself with this judgment to such an extent that you are interested in receiving congratulations on your small activities. This, presumably, is to encourage you to do more of them, as it is well understood that you can achieve nothing effective by doing so.

6

Brief essays – I

The belief in society

Now it is clear that before any change in human psychology, either individual or collective, could take place, it would be necessary for the belief in the meaningfulness of human society to be abandoned. (The resistance to its abandonment is of course immense.) It is true that this is only one of the attitudes which is invalidated by the perception of total uncertainty: but psychologically it is the lynchpin of the whole affair. If you *never* believe that human society, or collective opinion, can confer any meaningfulness upon your actions or attitudes, you can never develop the human psychosis in a permanent form.

Sub-societies

It is open to any subset of citizens in a capitalist society to form themselves into a communistic one, if they wish. They may decide to pool whatever financial resources they have, to confiscate surpluses from one another and redistribute them, and to submit themselves to any set of authoritarian restrictions they choose. The converse, however, is not true. It is not open to a member of a socialist society, or to any group of members, to decide that they would like to form a capitalist sub-society. The state is already confiscating their income and has already decided to what forms of authority they shall be subjected. This situation is not a reversible one.

Reality and social agreement

Even apart from specific psychological factors which may tend to distort perception of certain types of situation, there may be an underlying motivation in favour of the greatest possible discrepancy between the socially agreed view of any situation and the reality.

Objective reality is seen as a rival to social agreement about reality, and it is desired to assert the supremacy and superiority of the latter. The supremacy is most strongly asserted when it is in direct opposition to the facts.

One might see this as related to a psychological tendency to oppose the wishes of an excessively clever subordinate (e.g. person at school) on principle. However clever they may be and however much they think they know what is good for them, it is a way of asserting that one is still superior to them and more knowing than they are.

Life and death

Society wishes to possess the individual body and soul. It is easier to possess bodies than souls, so it is necessary for society to prove that there are no souls. This is why it is important to believe that psychology is an epiphenomenon of physiology, and why people are not allowed to commit suicide or take drugs. They are not allowed to express, in any way, any personal belief they may have that the continuation in physical life of their physical organism could, in any circumstances, be of subordinate importance to any other consideration. They are, of course, expected to regard their continuation in life as subordinate in importance to the purposes of society as soon as there is a war, but this is clearly a different matter. The important thing is that it should be impossible for any idiosyncratic assessment of the valuation of things to be allowed to take precedence over the priorities determined by society.

Category mistakes

Mr. Robert Maxwell observed that he did not like people who thought they were gentlemen, because they all had to use lavatory paper anyway. The logical status of this remark may be compared with: 'This vase asserts that it is red, not blue. I refute this presumptuous opinion by pointing out that it is round, not square.'

Category mistakes of this kind are perfectly acceptable in normal social life. They are only recognised by the human race in philosophy. That is to say, it is regarded as erroneous to ask: 'Where is consciousness?' (i.e. we should realise that consciousness is the sort of thing about which such questions cannot be asked). More accurately, we might say: we notice that consciousness belongs to the category of things about which, when we ask where they are located, we cannot give an answer. It should be observed that this does not solve, nor even illuminate, the problem of the relationship of consciousness to the physical world.

There is never anything wrong in asking questions: only in assuming that they necessarily have, or necessarily do not have, answers.

Friends and enemies

An enemy would rather pass himself off as a friend. It is an advantageous position. The friend has much greater claims to be allowed freedom of operation than the overt enemy; the harm that can be done is greater.

Even on the crudest level this is recognised. The enemy who approaches, shrieking threats at the top of his voice, is likely to find his victim fled.

Now it is a curious fact that very little serious consideration has ever been given to the idea that society may actually be hostile to individuals. It is accepted that individuals may be hostile to individuals; but that conglomeration of individuals called Society cannot, it seems, in its corporate actions, ever be so regarded.

The human psychosis

I have had occasion to converse with a certain number of socially labelled psychotics. The experience is very like trying to talk to a normal human being.

In the first place, their mental operations are clearly centred on *beliefs*. A socially labelled psychotic may *believe* he is being poisoned when he goes into restaurants, or persecuted by X-rays which make holes in the tin foil he keeps in his pockets. A normal human being *believes* in social agreement as the ultimate source of value.

Both types find these *beliefs* extremely interesting, and have no perceptible interest in facts. A psychotic, for example, is not in the least interested in discussing any facts which may bear upon the question of whether he is being poisoned in restaurants; a normal human is not interested in discussing whether social agreement is the ultimate source of value.

They are not only very interested in these beliefs, which they like continually reinforcing, but their interest in them is so great that they are scarcely interested in communications on any other point.

Workhouses

The contexts in which the human race is realistic about psychology are carefully selected.

In a 1932 propaganda film called *I am a Fugitive from a Chain Gang* we see the inadvisability of placing one's trust in agents of the collective. The escaped prisoner, lured to give himself up by promises from the powers-that-be of a pardon after three months, and a clerical job in prison, finds himself back in the chain gang and his pardon being deferred to an increasingly remote future. Very plausible, I'm sure. But the point of this piece of propaganda was not to warn everyone against the dangers of ever falling into someone else's power, but to accelerate the trend towards a state of society in which everyone would be dependent on trusting other people to have their interests at heart and provide for their needs in all the most essential matters of life.

Similarly, why did writers like Dickens and Charlotte Brontë permit themselves to portray cynically the psychology of those concerned in the running of charitable institutions? There was at least this to be said for the Victorian workhouse: nobody pretended that it was nice, or that you got into it if you could help doing so. And yet what we are rapidly tending towards is a society which is one vast glorified workhouse, in which it is sacrilege to suggest that anything preferable could possibly be obtained if one were free to purchase it with one's own money.

Human nature

With regard to my speculation about the psychodynamics of human nature — viz. that what makes people able to tolerate their own finiteness is positive appreciation of the finiteness of others. Well, it is a speculation. All that is really open to introspection is that interacting with people, or thinking about them, is what makes it hardest to be aware of the shockingness of the existential situation. People derive security and meaningfulness from other people. But the speculation arises, not from introspection, but because one observes that while people ostensibly set great store by other people, they don't really seem to mind about them much, at least about what happens to them.

Aesop

Among the Aesop's Fables that I read when I was five there was the one about the iron pot and the clay pot.

'I am so strong,' said the iron pot. 'Stick close by me and I will protect you.'

'Rather not,' said the clay pot (if it had any sense). 'You are so much stronger than I am that if there is any jostling along the way it won't be you that breaks.'

And I duly registered for future reference this warning against associating with those much more powerful than oneself. Curiously no one applies it to the state. But if an individual falls foul of the social mythology, a life can be destroyed in no time at all.

II: EVOLUTION AND CIVILISATION

7

Evolution and civilisation

The last significant change in the human race on a genetic level is supposed to have occurred some 50,000 years ago. From then on, we may suppose that the human inhabitants of this planet were of very much the type which inhabits it today. We may suppose that in that time there has been a certain amount of selection which would tend to develop and refine this type, by reference to its geographical environment and the circumstances of its life, and which would include selection for suitability to the social environment in which it found itself, whether tribal or some form of early civilisation.

Only at quite a late stage in this span of 50,000 years would there appear to have been much possibility of selection in favour of intelligence or the ability to handle abstract or numerical ideas. A society would have to have an alphabet and a system of commerce, including a coinage, before ability to handle such things would become favourable to survival in a consistent way. Circumstances of this kind arose (subject to certain variations and partial exceptions) only towards the end of the 50,000-year period. A few thousand years ago none of the modern European alphabets existed, and the picture alphabets which preceded them had much greater limitations.

So it appears that the length of time for which the human race can have been selected for its ability to survive in conditions at all comparable to those of a modern civilisation must have been very short in evolutionary terms. There seems little reason to suppose that the human population throughout the last 50,000 years of its history should be regarded as qualitatively different from ourselves. Whatever may be the highest flights of modern intellect, and whatever subtleties of emotional response and aesthetic appreciation may be found in modern populations, we must suppose that individuals with more or less equivalent potentialities were also being born in human societies before it was civilised in even the most primitive sense.

One conclusion we may draw from this observation is that human society has scarcely exploited to the full the potentialities for progress and development with which it has been provided by the genetic endowment of the most gifted individuals who occurred in its population. Crude picture alphabets and number systems arose for use in practical matters, but millennia passed without their being developed to the point where they became sophisticated enough to facilitate the development of communication of ideas, or much development in mathematics or science. Individuals must have been present who would have been capable of the intellectual analysis necessary to make such developments, but it would appear that the societies in which they lived were not constructed in such a way as to encourage, or even permit, the people who might have been able to make intellectual advances to have the freedom or incentive to do so.

8

Selection for social conformity – I

We may compare the rate at which control of the environment was increasing during the last 50,000 years with that which prevailed during two millennia of what we may call commercialist individualism from 0 to 2000 AD. Evidently the societies of the American Indians provided little opportunity for individual initiative to make itself felt. Without adequate written languages, language changed rapidly and communication between tribes was difficult. Even within them, the language was not stable and detailed information could not be retained.

One of the indications of a primitive language is that abstractions have not been made. For example, the Cherokee language had thirteen words, each of which corresponded to washing a different part of the body, but there was no recognition of the concept of washing as such, and no word for it. It is difficult to suppose that there had not been individuals within the Cherokee tribe who had the intellectual capacity to make such an abstraction and to perceive the usefulness of making it, but the social structure had provided no opportunity for individual perceptions of this sort to make any permanent contribution to the culture.

We may suppose that in this society selection in favour of intellectual ability was not very great, and rise in intelligence, if at all, occurred slowly.

On the other hand, we may suppose that selection for ability to conform to social pressures, of the kind that prevailed among American Indians, was relatively rapid. Males who failed in any way to demonstrate the required behaviour when called upon to expose themselves to pain and danger would soon be killed. We may confidently assume that any other form of deviant behaviour or rebellion against tribal norms would soon have encountered the ultimate solution.

A tribal society of this kind is slow to change. The rate at which it increases its control of the environment is slow, because individual intelligence and initiative in this direction are almost entirely eliminated. On the other hand, it is constantly selecting in favour of those personality types who are able to meet the requirements of the rigid (and demanding) lifestyle without rebellion or complaint.

9

Selection for social conformity – II

How has it come about that human psychology has the characteristics it has – characteristics that among other things lead it to tolerate, and even prefer, a 'welfare' state form of society, and to tolerate or even prefer a medical 'profession' of the current type?

Anything that can be called civilisation is relatively recent in genetic terms. The human race, perhaps even before it could be strictly speaking described as human, seems to have spent hundreds of millennia living in tribal groups. Can we see what psychological characteristics are likely to have been favourable to survival given the strategy adopted by groups of this sort?

Let us consider modern African pygmies, who tend to be regarded as rather lovely, and whose social arrangements do in fact offer a fair approximation to those of a modern socialist state, in that it is virtually impossible for any individual to choose for himself a lifestyle much different from that prescribed by the tribal norm, or to reduce his dependence on the goodwill of the group by any exercise of determination or ability.

Pygmy groups, rather like prides of lions, have a style of hunting which requires a minimum number of participants to be effective, so it is fairly reasonable that, so long as a person is in good enough health to keep up with the group and play his part, and refrains from breaking the social conventions, he can rely on at least a modest portion of the tribe's joint food supply. After the day's hunting and gathering, the men have a kind of communal musical evening from which women and children are excluded.

Until recent times any adult male member of the tribe sufficiently uninterested in demonstrations of social solidarity to be found asleep during the musical evenings was stabbed to death. Although this practice has been discontinued in modern times, it seems clear that genetic tendencies towards nonconformity have been discriminated against over a long period. A group of this kind has perpetuated itself by a form of co-operation in which no one can get more advantages for himself than the group is willing to give him; a desire for independence or autonomy would have been superfluous and possibly have led to any individual possessing it incurring group displeasure.

But we may note that the maintenance of such a system of group solidarity also requires that there be present in a sufficient number of the tribe a desire to punish non-conformity by stabbing, beating, ostracism, etc., and a lack of scruple about forcing members of the group to do whatever prevailing social opinion considers right and proper, even if this should happen to be against their will.

* * *

It is an extremely easy matter for a tribal society, in which the individual has little or no choice about the pattern of his lifestyle, to continue with little change for millennia. There is nothing an individual who dislikes the tribal customs and rituals can do about it. He cannot muster the economic power to liberate himself because there is no such thing as economic power, and he is as effectively subjugated as the population of an East European country during the communist era, in which any revolt is likely to be met by a massive array of armaments directed against it.

If the individual in a tribal society does not like what is expected of him it is quite likely that he will fall foul of the tribal requirements and his life expectation may be seriously diminished. The majority of human societies have not been slow to apply the death penalty or a near equivalent to any failure to conform. Since tribal societies can persist in much the same form for very long periods of time, we may suppose that this brings to bear a force of natural selection against those who are genetically inclined to social non-conformity, which might in other contexts be called independence or initiative.

Since so high a proportion of the cultures in which the human race has lived throughout its history have been tribal, in the sense of providing an extremely rigid framework within which the individual was forced to live, we may find it unsurprising that the desire to conform to the prevailing social ideals, and the desire to force others into subjugation to them, give every appearance of being extremely strong drives in human psychology.

10

Darwinism and society

In the case of an isolated animal, making its own way in the world, it is fairly clear what attributes will favour its survival. It will be subject to intense competition with other animals and to adverse circumstances, and its survival will depend on the realism and effectiveness of its reactions to these challenges. Sometimes an animal develops a characteristic which renders it almost immune to competition in certain respects, as an elephant by virtue of its size has little to fear from the attacks of other animals. Or circumstances, such as the geological accident of the land on which it is living becoming an island, may cut it off from the possibility of competition of certain kinds.

These forms of partial immunity are liable eventually to lead to weaknesses which are a source of danger if circumstances change. The elephant species is under little pressure to develop speed of reaction and other combative skills against predators which constitute a real threat to it; it might quickly become extinct if a lion of body mass approaching its own were to appear. The dinosaurs, by virtue of their size, also had little need to develop intelligence or other attributes, but were probably dependent on a certain climate and when it changed they had been protected for too long to find any effective response to the challenge of difficult conditions.

A tribal animal, such as man, is subject to two different forms of selective pressure. As an individual, when interacting with reality away from his tribe, and in certain circumstances in association with it, his survival is favoured by the usual factors: intelligence, forethought, grasp of reality, speed and effectiveness of response. Within the tribe he may be to a greater or lesser extent sheltered from these pressures, and his survival is favoured by other factors. The tribe as a unit is of course itself subject to the pressures of contact with reality; it must compete for territory and other advantages with any assailant tribe, or deal with any adverse climatic or other circumstance; but it may be able to shelter its members to a considerable extent from any need to react realistically.

The modern welfare state would undertake as far as possible to eliminate any selective pressure against its members on grounds of their inability to deal effectively with reality, or on account of weaknesses of physical constitution. Nevertheless social success within the tribe carries certain advantages, although the factors facilitating social success are less obvious than those relating to success in dealing with non-social reality.

Human beings are by so far the dominant species on this planet that tribes of them have been, for a long time, relatively free from certain realistic pressure. However, until recently (in geological time) tribal units had at least to react efficiently against other tribal units and against climatic and geological circumstances. By now, however, tribal units have expanded to fill land areas within boundaries, such as oceans and mountain ranges, which provide considerable hindrance to attack, so that war between tribes may be regarded as fairly exceptional, and the idea has developed that a tribe has some kind of natural right to the territory which it occupies. There is an aspiration in the direction of a single unified tribal unit, occupying the whole planet, and international organisations have been formed to reinforce these ideas of natural rights.

To the extent that it becomes realistic to regard the human race as a single tribal unit occupying the entire planet it will be in the position of a single species of dinosaur occupying an island on which there are no predators. The human race having gained a fair degree of control over disease and climatic conditions, there will be few external forces to penalise any preferences which the human race may have, or develop, for managing its affairs on principles other than those of effectiveness.

11

Tribes

Suppose that we believe in evolution. The picture which is presented to us by the history of the world is of life forms developing in an intensely selective way. Within an established species the mating rituals are often so severely competitive that only males with the greatest strength and stamina are able to breed at all. Each individual is subject to ruthless pressures from external reality, independently of the social pressures of selection within its own species. Predators are on the watch for the slow and sickly, and any mistaken interpreting of the environment or any lapse of attention may well be punishable by death.

At a fairly early stage of his development, man was in much the same position. He might be a member of a nomadic tribe, but the protection which it could offer him against predators, disease, and the hazards of climatic conditions was very limited. Inevitably selection proceeded in favour of physical robustness and intelligent forethought. Nowadays, when man lives as part of a very large tribe which has established a massive margin of control over the non-human reality, it is possible to debate the desirability of a 'work ethic' as though this was a dubious concept originated by puritanism or commerce. The original work ethic is simply that which is inherent in the struggle for survival against the forces of reality. He who does not build a strong fence will be eaten by wild beasts; he who does not dig his fields will have no crops; he who does not set his traps will have no meat to eat the next day. If you do not do the things which are necessary to keep yourself alive, you will not stay alive, whether the reason for your non-working is physical incapacity or a psychological preference for a less strenuous life.

However, as the human race developed it formed itself into groups and communities which were more complex and variable in their internal structure than those of other social and pack animals. This, combined with the fact that the human race, at least in places, started to develop a control over external reality, and methods of communicating among themselves so that information was not lost, started to create situations in which the forces of selection which influenced survival could be modified.

Even among pack animals such as wolves some aptitude for conformity to the social structure of the pack is necessary as well as skill in hunting prey. What is the fate which is likely to befall a wolf with an inadequate degree of social conformity? One may suppose that it may be torn to pieces or merely ostracized, and in the latter case perhaps it may break away from the pack and become an isolated hunter on its own. If it should meet another wandering wolf of the opposite sex, perhaps it may start a new pack of its own. In the days when there was plenty of uninhabited space in the world, it is easy to believe that many new tribes of humans were formed in the same way. If some early nomad felt himself very much at variance with the requirements of his nomadic group, so long as he was fairly competent in the skills necessary for survival, it was clearly open to him to break away, perhaps persuading his mate to go with him.

In those days perhaps it made more sense to talk of a 'social contract', since there was to some extent a real choice possible between remaining in the social group, with whatever requirements to conformity that entailed, and going away to live according to one's own lights. Now, of course, such a choice is scarcely possible. I, for example, find myself in a society where I may exercise one vote every four or five years in choosing between two groups of potential governors proposing slightly different packages of policies, both of which appear to be largely based on principles which I do not find at all attractive. But all the land in sight is under the jurisdiction of my tribe, and there is little of the world left where one would not be under the jurisdiction of one tribal society or another. So I do not think there is any real sense in which I can be said to have agreed to a social contract, by which I sacrificed some part of my autonomy in consideration of the benefits conferred upon me by having membership of this tribal group.

* * *

Richard Dawkins wishes to defend human culture from being regarded as the outcome of the same ruthlessly competitive forces that determine physiology, and also to some extent human psychology. Modern society likes to regard itself as 'altruistic', and to believe that it is demonstrating this attribute by making it socially acceptable for people to make donations to Oxfam. How has the current state of human culture actually come about?

So long as the human race was still in fairly direct contact with the non-social reality of the physical world, and so long as tribes were small enough and numerous enough to be in fairly constant conflict for territory and resources, it is clear that the culture of these tribes was itself subject to selective evolutionary pressures. Let us give a few very simple examples of the ways in which this worked, although in fact some of the factors concerned were probably far from obvious.

A tribe which set so high a value on artistic creativity that everyone spent their time painting pictures, on the cave walls or otherwise, and no one was available to procure food or fight off marauders, animal or human, would probably not survive long. When it came to a conflict between tribes, the culture and set of social values which produced the more efficient fighting force would clearly be at an advantage.

A tribe which insisted that everyone must play a precisely equal role in any undertaking, regardless of aptitude, would perhaps not do so well as what would today be called an 'elitist' tribe, which had its battle plans drawn up by those who had previously shown some ability for doing this instead of allocating this function at random.

A tribe which exposed and abandoned its surplus or disabled offspring, and left to starve those who were so old or feeble that they could no longer contribute to the maintenance of the tribe, might well survive longer as a tribe than another group which had a religious principle of keeping alive as long as possible all those who could be kept alive. In fact, it is not possible to give a historical example of an ancient tribe, or relatively primitive modern society, operating on the latter of the two sets of principles, and this may indicate that any group which attempted to do so soon died out. The burden of supporting the elderly and disabled would exhaust the energies of the able, and keep the whole tribe at a low subsistence level, which would leave it immediately vulnerable to any kind of unfavourable events.

* * *

Let us suppose there is a gene which mediates appreciation of high intelligence and a willingness to give it conditions in which it can work at gaining understanding of the environment. Actually the social forces which summate to create an appearance of these attitudes are probably more complex, but this does not affect the argument. A tribe in which this gene was plentiful would, other things being equal, soon be at an advantage in relation to other tribes.

A macroscopic example of this situation may be seen in the conquest of America by Europeans. Both North and South America had retained essentially the same tribal structures for millennia, and they were not, it would appear, structures which had offered much scope for potential scientists to come to the fore. European societies, on the other hand, for whatever reasons, had developed more complex and varied structures which, though perhaps only incidentally, permitted individuals to make and to communicate advances in controlling the forces of nature. So long as America was insulated from outside influences by its position as (in effect) a very large island, the tribes could only compete with one another without any one gaining overall dominance, although we may suppose that many tribes had been exterminated and enslaved by others in the course of these millennia of isolation. But when Europeans broke in upon this isolated situation, the technological superiority which they had gained (fairly recently, in relation to the long millennia of North American Indian tribal life) enabled them rapidly to gain control of the continent

It happens from time to time that an animal species finds itself in a situation where it is insulated from certain kinds of selective pressures. In this situation it is free to develop in what appears to it to be the most comfortable way. But this may leave it extremely vulnerable to any reintroduction of selective pressure at a later stage. Cf. Douglas Adams's New Zealand parrot (the kakapo), which had no predators for millennia, and eventually found itself with no inclination to run from predators.[1]

The human race has achieved a control of its environment which is so complete that it is effectively in this situation. All parts of the earth's surface are under the control of one massive tribal unit or another, so there is nowhere for any dissident to go to set up a competing tribal system. The existing tribes not only control the entire surface of the globe, but they have come to some sort of agreement among themselves to limit competition

---

[1] See Douglas Adams with Mark Carwardine, *Last Chance to See*, Heinemann, 1990.

with one another. Each tribe is now entitled to the territory which it has at present, and the tribes will unite to repel invasion by any tribe which fails to respect the boundaries of others. These conventions may not be perfectly adhered to, but we are at least in sight of a situation in which the total available area is dominated by a sort of super-tribe, which has eliminated competition between different areas of the world and adheres to some commonly agreed principles of morality. There is no question of invasion by some other human tribe, and the human race has achieved a technological ascendancy which places it in a position of complete dominance over other species of animal. The natural catastrophes which may arise within its territory also provide no serious threat to the continued existence and supremacy of the human race.

In these circumstances the human race is free to arrange its affairs in accordance with any ideology it sees fit, and this does not have to be the most efficient or the most survival-orientated. No comparison with alternative systems is going to arise, and the human race may, if it wishes, choose to use its very considerable safety margin to indulge in ways of arranging its affairs which utilise effort uneconomically and unprogressively.

In fact, in these circumstances, the human race appears to be choosing to adopt an egalitarian ideal, that is, one which nullifies, so far as possible, the forces of natural selection upon members of the human race, and also one which transfers the process of decision-making totally from the individual to a communal authority.

We have to ask how it has come about that this is what the human race has decided to do. Having evolved, like other animal species, in intensely competitive situations, what are the factors in its psychological evolution that apparently predispose it to choose to live according to principles of an egalitarian kind when the pressures upon it of non-social selective forces are all but removed?

12

The tolerance of oppression

What makes the human race so tolerant of oppression? Our ancestors must have lived in tribal societies for millions of generations, at any rate for far longer than the period of time during which at least some proportion of them have lived in societies which we might call civilised.

Civilisation begins with the concept of possession and the possibility of commerce; as it evolves it gives rise to increasing complexities of social structure, the possibility of greater variation in function and lifestyle, and the gradual refinement of a concept of respect for individual autonomy.

Success in a tribal society, in the sense of success in living long enough to produce viable offspring, depended on physical health, intelligence, compliance with the tribal norms, and the ability to tolerate a life in which there was not much scope for initiative, independent planning, or intensity of experience. It is easy to guess that boredom and depression would be best avoided by getting some influence over others, to make them comply better with the tribal requirements: killing and torturing enemies and wrongdoers, and whatever forms of communal jamboree were in favour.

It is not difficult to see the successful tribal personality in the sort of person able to tolerate the oppressions of modern collectivist society; they have not been selected for ambition and independence, and easily accept situations in which they have scope for neither.

But even if tribes in fact were as we have suggested, might not other types of tribe have evolved, which would have been just as successful but with a greater respect for individuality? Might not a cooperative society of independent, ambitious individuals be as successful, or even more so, in surviving as a group? Was there any logical necessity in the pattern of tribal groups of unambitious individuals, not very purposeful, highly tolerant of social oppression?

No doubt there were variations in the characteristics of different tribal groups, such as those between warlike American Indians and more peaceful, vegetative groups, but it would appear that until civilisation began, tribal groups rarely permitted much variation in lifestyle, and demanded a high degree of conformity to the tribal procedures. It seems to have been only with the start of civilisation, which depended on the development of a sophisticated idea of possession, that societies arose in which it was possible for independence and initiative to be used in a variety of ways, so that different personality types began to be favoured.

Once this process took place, however, societies which permitted individual variation and independence gained control of the environment more rapidly than those which did so less, and the former tended to take over the territories of the latter, so that the areas of civilisation spread and the areas of greatest civilisation spread their influence the most. This process, however, was reaching its culmination very recently with, say, the influx of

European influence into Africa and America. So the societies with the greatest scope for individuality seemed to be on the verge of global dominance. However, the terminus of European hegemony was in sight, leaving little scope for competition between societies with differing principles.

13

The evolution of meanness

A friend of mine made the experiment of asking some of her friends whether they did not think it serious that a genius might be impoverished and become unable to use his ability. A person who could really make use of money might not have it, and quite stupid people might have a lot, although nothing much could come of it. She was a bit surprised to find that a characteristic response was: 'It is much more regrettable that stupid people should have a lot of money than that a genius should not have it, and what does a genius want with money anyway?'

I am under the impression that this illustrates something fairly prevalent in human nature. From certain points of view it is in the interests of the human race to be preserved from this strange dimension of its psychological makeup (which we shall call 'meanness' for the sake of giving it a name), in the same way that it might be in its interests to have in the structure of its societies some restraint placed upon its tendency to produce unlimited quantities of offspring regardless of its ability to support them. The value of capitalism to the human race was that it preserved it from the full consequences of its own tendency to meanness, since it made it possible for some things to happen which people on the whole tended to find distasteful. If there is no check on meanness as an influence in social affairs, then of course society will evolve on different principles.

Let us consider what this dimension of meanness may be and what may be its evolutionary origins.

We perceive that the idea of taking away from people what they 'ought' not to have has a far stronger emotional loading than the idea of giving to someone that which he might need to function in the most productive way, or which he might need to be as happy as possible. The situation at which this motivation seems to be aimed – that of ensuring that no one has more freedom than they 'ought' to have on some egalitarian principle – is easily brought about. People are never so equal and unfree as when they are dead.

I remember reading a newspaper article about Sir Laurence Olivier. No doubt people tend to feel it is 'unfair' when someone is obviously better than everyone else in their field of activity, and when they have been marked out all their lives as 'good' at it, and have been able to achieve fame and fortune by the exercise of a talent which they presumably enjoyed exercising. At the time of the interview which I was reading about, Sir Laurence was old and frail. The journalist commented on the fact that, however great his talent had been, he was as subject as anyone else to mortality, with some such observation as this: 'When the king and the pawn are dismissed from the board at the end of the game, they are laid back in the same box.' I do not know whether people have a death wish on their own account, but it is easy to believe that they have it for anyone of whom they feel envious.

Even without going so far as to kill everyone, it is a fairly easy matter to set up a society in which it is virtually impossible for anyone to do anything but obey the dictates of his tribe, without any possibilities being open to him to do anything which might increase his freedom of choice.

It would appear that the human race has in large numbers, and for immense tracts of time, lived in forms of society which almost totally precluded the operation of individual initiative in forms other than those strictly prescribed by the tribal norms. Such societies have (so far as one can discover or guess, since many of them were prehistoric) been capable of great stability. We may plausibly guess that the rate at which developments were made in the control of the environment were far slower than they would have been if there had happened to be a slightly greater psychological inclination to admire exceptionally able people, and give them some freedom to make use of their abilities in such ways as occurred to them.

The kind of societies in which the human race appears to have spent the greater part of its historical past might well have the effect of selecting in favour of a strongly authoritarian moral sense, that is to say a strong emotional sense of what other people 'ought' to be made to do and 'ought not' to be allowed to. This would seem to go with a relatively weak inclination to use individual initiative. A tribal society whose members have a strong sense of the righteousness of the tribal ideal, and little inclination to pursue individualistic aims, has certain advantages from the point of view of survival as a tribal group.

Nevertheless, undemanding submission and conformity, combined with a strong desire to inculcate these qualities in others, are not the only qualities which favour the survival of the group. In the great and classic confrontation between the emerging capitalism of Western Europe and the more static societies of the rest of the world, the advantages of control over the environment were clearly demonstrated. The American Indians, for example, formidable as they were in hand-to-hand fighting, and totally dedicated as they may have been to the warlike ideals of their tribes, were no match for Europeans armed with guns, which had been developed by the growth of scientific knowledge, made possible by a commercial society which permitted inequality of property.

* * *

We have given some indications of the advantages of the individualistic West in the relatively recent rise to dominance of commercially oriented societies. But how would this work on a more primitive level? Before science was developed, what advantage could there be to a tribe in having a permissive or favourable attitude towards cleverness?

So long as tribes occupied small areas of land, or were nomadic, there would be some selective pressure in favour of less mean attitudes. Clever people, even if you did not like them, might think of better weapons or better defences. Even improvements in your methods of growing food or storing it might place you at an advantage when you had to fight off another tribe. But as soon as you reach a situation in which you are free from frequent conflicts with other tribes, because you have entered a territory free from other human inhabitants, or because you have expanded your tribal territory to some natural barrier such as an ocean or a mountain range, you can settle down and indulge your tribal meanness to the full, setting up a thoroughly restrictive and moral society in which everyone may derive a good deal of their entertainment in life from making sure that everyone else keeps the rules and does not have more of anything than they deserve.

So now the last great possibility confronts the human race; to fill the whole world with a social pattern which can never be challenged. And is this to be – as we would like it to be – one in which clever people should never have more than the average?

14

Jealousy and evolution

Jealousy of the most destructive kind is a characteristic that has a good deal going for it from an evolutionary point of view. Social and economic success and status are very likely to increase the scope of an individual for producing offspring and providing for them in such a way that they are likely to survive. If you are a peasant struggling to survive and keep your children fed in Siam, you may worry about the King of Siam with his hundreds or thousands of legitimate and illegitimate, more or less pampered, offspring. They are going to be there in the next generation competing with your offspring for whatever opportunities and resources are available in Siam.

But does it matter if a high proportion of the King of Siam's genes occur in the next generation, so long as the size of the overall population remains constant? If the King of Siam is responsible for a very high proportion of the next generation, and the peasant population only for a very few, will this actually make the chances of your own peasant offspring any worse, compared with a situation in which the King of Siam produced only the same percentage of the new population as did the average peasant?

The situation will actually be worse for your offspring the better, in competitive terms, the King of Siam's genes are. If he is strong, clever, and energetic, his offspring may compete far too effectively with your own offspring, and your chances of bringing your own offspring to maturity will be reduced. So it is actually a good idea, from the point of view of the survival of your genes, to obstruct the progress of anyone that you seriously suspect of being more able and competent than yourself. It will matter far less that the King of Siam contributes a disproportionate number of surviving offspring, if you can be sure that he is a feeble and stupid person.

Let us always remember that it is not the absolute goodness of genes which counts; it is whether they are still there in the population some generations later. And the point of the complex social structures devised by humans is that social selective pressures can be added to those which are provided by the struggle with external reality.

It is true that if jealousy functions too efficiently in a given tribal group in restricting the procreation of its most able and energetic members, there may come a time when this tribe no longer functions well enough in competition with some other tribe, or in coping with natural catastrophes. It may then have reduced itself to a collection of dull and idle people with no interests but food, sex, and trivial amusements, these being the sort of people by whom everybody feels least threatened.

There seems little doubt that jealousy, and the obstructing of persons of superior ability to one's own, would appear to have some evolutionary value from the point of view of the survival of one's own genes. But so long as tribal groups were subject to external selective pressures, we may suppose that some sort of balance was maintained between this psychological factor and others which were more conducive to the promotion of ability. By now, as pointed out earlier, the human race has arrived at a 'large island' situation. The pressures of external reality, and of competition with other societies running their affairs on different principles, are remote, and there is little to check the effective operation of jealousy as a force in human society. The technological advances which have been contributed by some of the most able members of the human race provide an immense buffer of security. It could be that at some remote date in the future, a universal plague will arise and the human race will no longer contain sufficient members who are capable of understanding the traditional principles of biochemistry well enough, or of devising organisational procedures effective enough, to combat it. But plainly this possibility is so far in the future that it need be of no concern to anyone.

Quite possibly the evolutionary origin of jealousy is connected to the fact that superior ability is far more deeply resented than mere wealth. Wealthy winners of football pools, even wealthy pop stars and tennis players, seem to be subject to a less profound hostility than hereditary aristocrats or persons with high IQs. While it is acceptable to describe aristocrats as 'brainless' and 'chinless', I have a suspicion that they would be better tolerated if they genuinely fit this description. In fact at least some of their ancestors must have reached their position by some kind of effective success in the past, and a person with an aristocratic background, while not necessarily superlatively intelligent, continues to be more effective for a good many purposes (statistically speaking) than a person without it. It is difficult, of course, to say how far this is due to inherited qualities and how far to upbringing, but at least so long as they are able to continue providing their offspring with advantageous attitudes, they are not likely to be regarded as desirable competitors.

15

Jealousy and king-killing

Direct observation of the human race has never given me a strong feeling that altruism was a particularly dominant feature of it.

So how does it come about that, although capable of considerable indifference, if not more or less obvious malice towards any individual that he may encounter, a modern person frequently subscribes to the view that *altruism* has become the dominant factor in human affairs on a macroscopic scale? In practice he is unlikely to consider himself in sufficiently favourable circumstances in life to do more than eat an ostentatious bread-and-cheese lunch from time to time (for the benefit of the starving millions), and his altruism is more likely to express itself with any emotional force in his concern that others, who are richer than he is, should not be allowed to give lavish parties instead of using their resources to succour some dwellers in cardboard boxes who could readily be found in the vicinity. This, of course, probably provides the key to the situation. What is being expressed is not altruism at all, in the sense that this person has any serious desire that anyone should have more freedom than they do, but rather a desire that those who do have some should be dragged down to the level of those who do not. I think human psychology is sophisticated enough for us to suppose that communal expressions of 'altruism' are perceived as a socially acceptable and effective way of expressing jealousy. Human history, even extremely recent history, contains little to suggest that human beings have any reliable inhibition against causing one another suffering, or any reliable tendency towards generosity even in circumstances where it is perfectly plain that someone else could be made a good deal happier by it. The cultural importance attached to 'altruistic' ideals, such as injunctions to 'love one another', have led to little definition of such ideals, and certainly not of any kind that hindered their being freely interpreted in terms of whatever might be the prevailing forms of social oppression.

If your genes are to be successful in the competition for survival, you will need to have one or both of two related drives. You will want to be more successful than other people at gaining all the things which will conduce to the survival of your offspring, and you will also wish to ensure that no one can be more successful than you are. A person who has the genes to be a good competitor represents a threat, and it is particularly desirable in that case to ensure that he does not achieve success.

Success is likely to mean opportunity to produce many offspring and, particularly as societies become more complex, opportunity to ensure survival in favourable circumstances for many of those offspring. What is more, those offspring will themselves have a share of these good, competitive genes. Your own offspring will therefore be competing against a large number of well set-up people who are likely themselves to be quite good competitors.

Does this provide any clue to the strength of jealousy in human society, especially perhaps the tendency to assassinate the prominent and successful, although this may appear to be accounted for by the political views of the assassin? Does it, perhaps, provide us with a clue to the prevalence of traditions of the *Golden Bough* type? After the king's temporary rule he is killed and replaced, this being typically explained by some belief in the fertilising value of his body. The beliefs in the advantage of this practice are not true, and tribes which practiced it were not really rewarded with more bountiful harvests. But, supposing the king to be selected for genuine ability, the genes of those who practiced such a system would be rewarded by fewer able competitors in the next generation.

However, we may suppose that if a tribe carried out the practice of sacrificing its most able members too far, the quality of the group as a whole might be significantly reduced, so that its chances of survival as a group in conflict with some other group would be reduced.

So long as we are thinking of the intra-tribal situation rather than an inter-tribal one, it seems possible that it will be advantageous for the survival of your genes if you can produce as many offspring as possible and ensure that the competitive ability of other future members of the tribe is as low as possible. So we see that there may be quite a strong genetic disposition in the direction of directing any altruism you may feel to the benefit of the least adequate competitors, while you may well be motivated not to promote the interests of the able and indeed to find ways actively to hinder them.

This possible genetic rationale appears to correspond very well with those tendencies in human psychology which are readily apparent in everyday social life, and indeed have given rise to the ideology associated with the formation of a 'welfare state'. But while this may be true, these psychological tendencies have never before been able to set up a situation in which they were, to so great an extent, released from the check of any counterbalancing influences. The fact that human genetic tendencies may find expression in the establishment and implementation of modern ideals of egalitarianism is no guarantee of the long-term viability of such a situation. The selective processes which have acted upon the genes determining human psychological dispositions may well have selected in favour of genes favouring attitudes of jealousy and egalitarianism, but they have not selected for ability to survive effectively in a welfare state environment. There has never before been a situation in which the selective forces in favour of competence, responsibility and forethought could be to so considerable an extent negated.

Indeed, we may wonder whether the selective forces which might favour such qualities have not effectively been reversed. It is not only that it has been made equally easy for all members of the population to reproduce, regardless of their competence in supporting their offspring, but it may have been made differentially discouraging for the able, responsible and forethoughtful to reproduce, so that their genes will be proportionally less represented in each succeeding generation. It has been pointed out that the birth rate has fallen among the most highly educated. In the past there may have existed selective pressures in favour of a gene which instructed its owner to have only so many children as he or she could see their way to supporting and educating. People with such a gene may well find themselves disinclined to reproduce in circumstances in which it is difficult to gain sufficient financial resources to afford a proper education; whereas persons with genes which instruct them to have as many children as possible and hope for the best, regardless of the future prospects and upbringing of these hapless children, would presumably find no deterrent in a situation where their children's upbringing and some semblance of education were guaranteed, not by their own ability to provide it in accordance with their own principles and standards, but by the state.

16

Women in tribes

Let us consider how the characteristics of human psychology may derive from the structure of tribal society.

There is no 'drive to infinity', or drive towards any goal outside the tribal group. There is no concerted attempt to increase control of the environment, nor is it possible for any individual to make wholehearted attempts to better his own lot. The object of everything is to reinforce belief in the importance of the tribal customs, so that the people in the tribe can live out their life cycles according to these patterns, often with little change for centuries or millennia.

There is relatively more scope for the men to assert their own significance by means of aggression towards something external to the tribe, since they have from time to time to defend the tribe from the encroachments of other tribes, and probably to kill animals for food. This kind of assertion takes the form of proving that they are able to deprive another being of its life, i.e. that on behalf of the tribe they are able to assert their superior potency by this act of depriving. Nevertheless, this relatively externalised assertiveness gives male psychology its slight margin of generosity and flexibility.

The women, on the other hand, having no way of asserting themselves outside the tribe, and concerned with the bringing up of children, have no outlet for their drive except in the satisfaction they can obtain from subordinating the children, and no doubt everybody else as well, to the tribal customs. (One can hear the tribal echoes in many common expressions: 'She must be *helped to adapt* to a non-academic life', 'She must be brought into subordination to the tribal customs.')

17

Brief essays – II

Derivation of values from groups

I think it is generally accepted these days that plural quantities of human beings are very important, and that an individual placed in such a plural quantity, called a group, comes to derive his values from whatever the consensus is in the group.

When I think of any group which I have known, none of them actually seems to me so attractive that I could have wished to derive my values in life from them, but I think that what is true is that being exposed to a group situation can make it extremely difficult for a person to maintain his identification with any values which the group does not possess. This, I suppose, is one of the standard procedures in brainwashing. It must also be particularly efficacious with children; you may think of the Dauphin of France deprived of all contact with his relations and exposed to the society of revolutionaries who had been instructed to indoctrinate him in the revolutionary outlook.

No doubt it was too difficult for him to maintain his identification with his parents' standards, and difficult also to realise that such concessions as he made in behaviour to his gaolers' demands were made only under pressure, and probably he was thoroughly demoralised before ill health or poison gained the upper hand.

Goodwill

There is usually no evidence of 'goodwill' in human relationships apart from certain verbal expressions. These have a number of distinctive forms.

If, for example, you were marooned on the Arctic ice, sending up flares to attract attention to your plight, and a human being happened by in his ship, by analogy one might expect him to say, 'That was a nice flare you sent up just then,' or, 'You must get a lot of satisfaction out of sending up flares,' or 'Nice little camp you have here on the ice.'

After these expressions of 'goodwill' he would sail on, without enquiring whether you had any interest in being removed from your ice floe.

Caring

The concept of whether anyone cares about anyone else is emotionally loaded in a curious way, and it is necessary for the adult psychotic to acquire an extremely complicated and contradictory system of attitudes and beliefs on this point.

For example, it is a fairly clear feature of normal life that no one will actually stir an inch out of their way to help anyone else (except in so far as purely ritual actions are dictated by social convention). For anyone to become a socially acceptable member of society, it is necessary for him to realise clearly that however dire his needs, he must not make the slightest claim on anyone else that they should be recognised. At any rate he must act according to this belief, whether or not he is conscious of it. And yet, at the same time, he is expected to utter a good many assertions about the benevolence of everyone in particular and society in general.

The mother of a friend of mine once told her (she was then in her teens) that when people asked after her affairs, she should not answer at great length, because they were not really interested. She had to understand that no one else was really interested in her, they were only pretending to be. At the same time her mother told her that she should take more interest in other people – that is, when she met them, she should be sure to ask them a good many questions about themselves, to which they would reply only briefly, because of course they knew that she had no real interest in them.

Relationships

The essential and underlying feature of all relationships is that no one will do anything for you. They will not give you money, however urgent your purposes may be. They will not even lend you money, however little it might inconvenience them, and however great the inconvenience from which it might save you. A relationship is a kind of interaction in which you do not refer to these facts, and thank one another profusely for extremely small pieces of 'help', which are usually, on analysis, harmful. It is not quite clear why doing this should be supposed to be interesting.

Compassion

It is alleged that a wicked judge, sentencing a man who had stolen a loaf, replied to his explanation that he had to live, 'Je n'en vois pas la nécessité.' More recently, it was alleged that an ex-servant said that there would be no servant problem if people stopped wanting servants.

Both remarks, if true, demonstrate the psychological verity (which there are, quite independently of these particular remarks, no grounds whatever for doubting) that human beings have no noticeable awareness of one another's needs. Not, that is to say, any awareness that expresses itself in a tendency to supply those needs. In a certain sense, however, they may be said to have an awareness. If you should ever find yourself hanging from a precipice by your fingertips and a fellow human being happens by, be careful what you say. If he realised your position he might tread on your fingers.

Beethoven's housekeeper

Beethoven had a housekeeper. She did the cooking and housekeeping while he composed music. I am sure the modern view of the matter is that Beethoven did not need a housekeeper, or, if he did, he should not have done. Plainly, they should both have composed music, and both have cooked their own meals. The fact that Beethoven composed music better than the housekeeper could have done is beside the point. It is the business of society to iron out these unfair advantages of endowment, not to enhance them. Why should the housekeeper not have had just as much chance to practise creative self-fulfilment? It is interesting to observe that the housekeeper could probably have composed music just as well in the intervals of her cooking and housekeeping as she could have done if she had had all day free to devote to thinking about the music. Beethoven, on the other hand, probably could not have composed nearly as well as he did if he had had to do so part-time. This proves that the housekeeper had a better social adjustment than Beethoven, and is all the more reason why Beethoven should not have received preferential treatment.

Money

One of my aphorisms is as follows:

'No one says: The infinite is infinitely important; nothing in the world is more than finite, therefore it is easy to act uncompromisingly. The nearest they get to this is: Nothing is very important, so there is no point in being uncompromising.'

A somewhat similar situation prevails in relation to money (possibly it is a psychological corollary of the more general statement).

Nobody says: Money is not very important, but I see that you want it, so I will give you some of mine. Everybody says: Money is not very important, so you should not want it, and I will see that you don't get any of mine.

III: THE BASIC MORAL PRINCIPLE

18

The basic moral principle – I

Modern society has lost sight of the only moral principle of any importance, so that the individual citizen is basically unprotected against unlimited oppression.

Since the ignored principle is never enunciated, it is difficult to express one's horror at what already goes on, and at even worse developments that might go on. If someone says, 'People ought to be heavily taxed in order to pay for state-administered medicine and education', I am shocked and horrified, but inhibited from replying: 'People ought to be taxed as little as possible, and certainly not at all to provide funding for organised crime.'

Usually I do not reply in this way, because I realise that prolonged explanation would be necessary. In reality, at least as much explanation should be required to make plausible the idea that individuals should be taxed to provide for greater oppression of individuals by the collective, but one realises that a high proportion of the population has learnt to proceed smoothly to this conclusion without examination, or even recognition, of the underlying assumptions being made.

If I say that people should be taxed as little as possible, and least of all to finance collectively organised oppression, this depends on the basic moral principle that society should interfere as little as possible with the individual's freedom to evaluate for himself the various factors which affect his existential situation, and to react to it as effectively as his resources permit.

The basic moral principle applies between individuals as well, and everyone should respect the right of others to evaluate for themselves the weighting to be placed on the factors which enter into any given situation, since in reality the existential situation is one of total uncertainty.

However, it is only socially appointed agents of the collective, such as doctors, teachers, social workers, etc, who are invested with legally conferred powers to impose their valuations on others. They should be deprived of these (immoral) powers.

In fact, in the presence of the modern ideology, the deplorable practice has arisen of taking into account only factors which appear obvious to a large number of people, and of assuming that any others should be ignored.

In place of the basic moral principle enunciated above, an alternative one is implicitly assumed. This is apparently an idea to the effect that what is ethical consists of what the majority of people agree to regard as ethical. Dissenting individuals can and should be forced to submit to the views accepted by the majority of people in their society.

As people are subjected to continuous indoctrination in modern society, from the educational system, which increasingly regards indoctrination as a primary objective, and from the continuous stream of propaganda being put out by such media as television and newspapers, it is not surprising that nearly universal tendencies to prefer currently fashionable ways of evaluating things are to be observed.

We may suppose that similar unanimities of evaluation were usually found in primitive tribal societies, notwithstanding that a member of modern society, under the influence of the prevailing ideology, would regard some of the practices of primitive societies as immoral. This does not present itself to the modern mind as a problem, since there is an implicit belief that the human race has recently arrived at the best possible way of evaluating things, and the way it thinks now is unquestionably right.

Given the basic moral principle that the freedom of the individual to form his own evaluations is supremely important, even if in practice the majority of people will adopt the valuations suggested by the ideology which prevails in the culture of their place and time, the functions of society acting on a collective basis should be as limited as possible. As Herbert Spencer suggests, they should be limited to what is necessary to protect the liberty of individuals from encroachment by other individuals.

19

The basic moral principle – II

Having stated the basic moral principle, it can be seen how freely it is violated in modern society.

What destroyed my education, and has made it impossible for me to recover from the effects of that destruction ever since, was not *au fond* the hostility and oppressiveness of any particular individuals, but the intrinsic immorality of the modern ideology. My parents were operating in an environment in which there was no shortage of people to prescribe to them how they should regard me.

The legislation which prevented the taking of the School Certificate and other exams before a certain age was a clear violation of the basic moral principle. It was denying to the individual who might be taking exams, or to his parents who were supposed to be considering his interests, the right to evaluate for himself how serious were the advantages or disadvantages, in an existential perspective, and in view of his individual characteristics and outlook, of taking an exam of a certain kind at a particular age.

People's lack of sensitivity to this basic principle of morality, even so soon after the Second World War when the welfare state had been in force for only a few years, was shown by the fact that even supposedly conservative newspapers found no fault with the legislation. Protests were made on behalf of a few children who were clearly going to be prevented from taking exams that they were well able to take, but newspaper articles which discussed such individuals were only too willing to impose solutions of their own, on the lines of 'If he/she is so clever, he/she can easily pass the time reading books/playing chess/doing good works.'

This shows that the willingness to impose solutions and interpretations on other people's lives was already well developed. No doubt it always has been, and that is why there is little hope of the basic moral principle being upheld, except in a free-market society in which an individual can defend himself against other people's ideas of what he ought to want by paying with money for what he does want.

Of course, the young person is necessarily at a disadvantage so long as he has to depend on decisions being made on his behalf by a parent, and even more so if he is dependent on decisions being made by someone who has not even some sense of genetic bonding with him. One of the things which would have saved my education from complete disaster, so that its inverse could be said to be the cause of its ruin, would have been an age of legal majority which was related to mental rather than chronological age. On the most conservative estimates of my IQ, I would certainly have been of age and free to make decisions for myself before the School Certificate situation arose.

Clearly those most likely to be disadvantaged by the age-limit legislation were the most precocious (in those days it was not yet explicitly stated that there was no such thing as precocity). So this legislation conveyed to all and sundry that there was no need to take into account any special individual requirements that might arise from special ability. This was treated as implying also that the possibility of any special needs arising from unusually extreme individual characteristics should not on any account be entertained.

The latter is pretty much the principle that has been applied to me throughout my life. Could it be that people realise that ignoring the particular requirements which arise from outstanding ability is a good way of providing it with the handicaps which are desirable to cancel the likelihood of its possessor being able to make use of it? Of course by now it has become acceptable to assert that there is no such thing as precocity or outstanding ability anyway. At that time people liked to refer gloatingly to cases of child prodigies who had 'fizzled out'. The implication of this was not that they had not retained their ability, but that some strange innate deficiencies had rendered them unfunctional in later life. From time to time throughout my life, including quite recently, I have read newspaper articles quoting educational 'experts' as remarking on the number of early high achievers who finish up without an academic career. This is supposed to constitute a proof that this is a perfectly natural outcome, but it might just as well be taken as a demonstration of the hostility towards them, and their consequent inappropriate treatment by the educational system.

Some twenty years ago, in connection with the then fashionable proposals for the further deterioration of the university system, Professor Andrew Oswald of Warwick University was quoted as saying, 'Why exactly should Britain's plumbers and secretaries and telephone operators have to pay for you to come to Warwick? You will earn far more than them. You will have much more interesting jobs.'[2] This shows how hopeless it is to expect the state to provide for the differing needs of individuals. In reality, there are many factors, of which measurable IQ is only one, which affect the circumstances and types of activity which an individual needs for his well-being. It is impossible to quantify the weighting of these factors in an individual case, and it is a violation of the basic moral principle to impose conditions on him which take into account only very few factors.

And, supposing (as I do) that IQ and other innate characteristics strongly influence the individual's aptitudes and temperament, let us remember how heavily outnumbered by the majority of the population at large is the minority (about 3%) even with IQs above 130, at which level a child is (or used to be) referred to as 'gifted'. Really outstanding IQs, at a level which used to be described as 'near genius' or 'potential genius', constitute a tiny minority of the 'gifted' population. So how can it possibly be expected that a democratic society will provide adequately for the needs of, say, the top 1% of the population, of whom the remaining 99%

---

[2] *The Times*, 31 May 2000.

are jealous, and whose success and well-being they resent?

20

Free markets and the basic moral principle

The only alternative to paying for what you want is to be dependent on what other people see fit to provide you with, which is a violation of the basic moral principle, since their evaluations are thereby imposed on you.

It has been particularly clear in my life that you cannot expect people to be aware of what is in your interests, or to promote them if they are. People have had no sympathy with me at any age. If you say people have always behaved as if they were in a conspiracy to make my life a perfect misery and obstruct me as far as possible, that describes it pretty well. The only exception to that was the convent school I attended, where the outlook was not fully in line with the prevailing ideology; and, to a less positive extent, the private preparatory school which I went to earlier, which did not teach me anything but provided a reasonably pleasant and civilised environment where I was treated as well as anyone else. But that was an environment which my parents purchased with money.

As for conspiracy, I know how strongly taboo it is to mention the possibility, but on my observations it is very easy for people to behave as if in a conspiracy, as they all interpret things and react to them in the same ways.

Although the effect of a concerted and co-ordinated attack may be produced, I do not believe they communicate explicitly with one another on the lines of: 'People who are obviously precocious can have their lives destroyed by universal refusal to admit the reality of their ability, or of any associated needs to do things which would not be possible if the ability were not there'. Similarly, when one had become an academic in exile, cast out from the only sort of career one could have, there is a universal refusal to consider the unnaturalness of this situation, and positive opposition to any action on the part of the outcast that would constitute moving in the direction of re-entry into an academic position with suitable status and salary.

So my strongest needs and deprivations have gone unrecognised throughout my life, and I do not have the slightest hope of benefit accruing to me from anyone's evaluation of my interests, which is more likely to do me harm than good.

Although the case of a high-IQ person is a particularly obvious one, and it is possible to account for nearly all features of modern society as determined by hostility to ability, history provides little reason to think that it is, in general, in any way natural for people to act benevolently to one another, and plenty of reason to think that there is little in human genetic programming to prevent them from treating one another as cruelly as possible.

This is only to be expected since the evolutionary situation is competitive, as with any successful animal species, and it is in the interests of the individual's future representation in the gene pool, not only that he stays alive, but that he does down the competition, who are producing offspring with which his own will learn to compete. The most effective and threatening (in the sense of superior functionality) are to be particularly discriminated against, but there is limited reason for generosity towards anyone.

But must this be counterbalanced by some tendency towards solidarity with members of the tribal group? A tribe whose members had no inclination to rescue fellow tribesmen in distress would become numerically depleted and lose out in conflicts with stronger tribes. Some sort of balance has presumably been set up; but who are going to be the most useful tribal members? Not the bright, not the enterprising, not those who are clever at knowing their own interests as individuals, or defending them if they know them. Those to whom social conformity is all will do best for strengthening the tribe; the solidly bovine who will do as they are told and uncomplainingly hew wood and till fields, and join in group activities in defence of the tribe when necessary – unrebellious cannon fodder, or spear-and-club fodder.

The belief that there are no internal determinants of behaviour is a useful tool in reinforcing hostility to those who do possess internal determinants to a noticeable extent. So, since it is believed that there is no such thing as innate giftedness, and no such thing as genetically determined drive or ambition, it was considered justifiable to hold my parents responsible for the occurrence of both those things in me, and since these characteristics were supposed to be the products of some social influence, they did not have to be respected as permanent factors to be taken into account.

21

'Rights' in the modern world

The invention of 'rights' is a very popular feature of modern social oppression. It would be easy to lose sight of the fact that they have no basis in reality, nor even in the long-term traditions of the human race. Every right, such as the right of every child to spend the early years of its life in a school, corresponds only to something that the majority of people who have been brought up within the modern religion considers desirable; and each of them corresponds to an additional confiscation of freedom from individuals and a transfer of power to agents of the collective, who will administer these rights in accordance with their understanding of the will of the collective. As these rights are set up, other rights, which some might consider more important, fall into oblivion; such as, for example, the basic and overriding principle that an individual has a right not to have his liberty infringed except in so far as he is infringing the liberty of others.

It may be easy enough to agree that human beings should have a 'right' not to be imprisoned without cause, and a very serious and clearly demonstrated cause at that, and that they should not be tortured or starved when they are in prison. This comes from the basic principle of respect for the liberty of the individual, but even such simple rights as these can scarcely be regarded as securely based. Even in the most civilised parts of the world – that is, where respect for the volition of the individual has been reinforced for some centuries by a free market system – an individual has been able to consider himself free from capricious imprisonment and physical maltreatment for relatively few human generations, and the signs are that the principle is being eroded rather than the reverse, as society comes to consider itself free to do people good or, in its estimation, to prevent them from doing harm to themselves, by violating their wills.

Thus, some fifty years ago, a female undergraduate suspected of suicidal tendencies was taken by the principal of her college, on a dishonest pretext, to a mental hospital where she was incarcerated and forced to lie in a bed under bright lights which could not be turned off. If this could happen fifty years ago, I feel sure that similar violations of the will are even more likely to be perpetrated today. And then there is the imprisonment of children whose parents are suspected of having maltreated them in some way.

Examples of the ease with which these principles can be blurred even in the most civilised of present-day societies could be multiplied, but let us instead turn to considering what is the real effect of promoting the idea that a freedom from imprisonment and torture must be accepted as a human right on a global basis. The effect is certainly not that attention is turned on refining the stringency of this principle in parts of the world where it is already vaguely accepted, nor on preventing its erosion by the increasing presumptions of society in the direction of doing good to its members while losing sight of the need to refrain from doing them harm. Instead, attention is focused on the exhortation to reform of various parts of the world where these principles, even in the crudest form, are clearly and freely violated.

I do not know how much manpower is employed, or at what cost, to exert pressure in these areas. But no doubt a good deal of money could be expended in this way without achieving very significant effects. So a good deal of freedom could be taken away from the citizens of this country in order to attempt to instil into other parts of the world a crude and rudimentary respect for individual liberty which has been achieved in this country as the outcome of several centuries of commercial activity with its accompanying ethos of respect for human property.

A commercial society must have clearly defined concepts of individual property, and as in the long run this leads to individuals being able to buy not only goods but services according to their own choice, it leads eventually to an ethic of respect for the volition of the individual. This, however, is a slow process. We may say that the Victorians were beginning to have a glimmer of an idea of respect for the individual, but now the trends of modern ideology are against it. The modern version of respect for the individual is as follows. The individual should have as much freedom as the society in which he lives considers he has a right to, in a society where the agents of the collective have as much power as they need to have, to make society turn out as the sort of society that the majority of people who have been brought up in such a society will consider as providing everyone with what they ought to have a right to.

22

Tribalism and ethics

The essential feature of ethics – that is to say, respect for the right of the individual to have what he wants and to decide for himself what is of importance to him, so long as it is not interfering with the rights of others to pursue what they consider important for them – arose in association with capitalism. It was an ethic that could only arise when individuals had at least the potentiality of paying for what they wanted within the structure of the society they lived in.

This ethic has been nominally subsumed within the modern trend towards tribalism. We will retain the great advances in knowledge and control of our environment which were made when collective control was somewhat weakened, but we will not consider it moral for individuals to pursue whatever goals they consider conducive to whatever sort of wellbeing they choose for themselves, unless we happen to agree with them. ('We' is a vague collective entity consisting of social agreement about what is right and proper.)

We aim to remove freedom, so far as we can, but we sweeten the pill by confirming our belief in the 'individual'. Indeed, we respect the 'individual' more than ever before and complain that the previous state of society had too little of this respect. But when the nature of this 'respect' is formulated, it does not come out to anything so simple and absolute as respect for other people's power to decide; it comes out as a concern for their well-being, based on some sort of 'balanced' assessment of their total wants and needs. By implication this is an assessment that *we* will make, not they, and 'balance' provides a lot of scope for overriding a person's strongest inclinations if our respect for them is 'balanced' by our respect for something else that they should be inclined to want instead.

23

Brief essays – III

The wisdom of the tribe

There is nothing enormously original in the idea that the state or the tribe will wisely and collectively provide the individual with the opportunities and understanding that he ought to want. If he should happen to be unhappy it is his own fault; the state or the tribe or the priests of the gods are quite prepared to help him understand where his true happiness lies. Probably such arguments could be heard in ancient Egypt, among the American Indians and in tribal situations even earlier.

Thus you have the idea that the tribe is intrinsically 'good' and the agent of the tribe is intrinsically 'good'. So if you happen to point out that a certain qualified doctor has actually done something damaging, or a certain properly certified teacher, you are likely to be told that he or she just happened to be 'a bad doctor' or 'a bad teacher' and no inferences should be drawn from this about doctors or teachers in general. You cannot use it to argue for a situation in which the individual has greater powers of decision and doctors or teachers less. What is clearly present to everyone's mind is the advantages that will accrue if the right sort of doctors and teachers have greater powers of decision than individuals.

Max Frisch's *Andorra*

The moral of Frisch's play is supposed to be 'Thou shalt not make graven images'. The idea, apparently, is that if you have preconceptions about what people of various races, etc., must be like, you are not leaving them freedom to be what they are, and the consequences are liable to be tragic. In the play the central character, called Andri, is falsely supposed by everyone to be a Jew and treated accordingly. He is told that he is different from the others, has more intellect than feeling, and is more suited to salesmanship than to manual work as a carpenter. Needless to say, he protests in the most appealing manner that he positively dislikes being thought cleverer than other people, desires nothing except to be exactly identical with everybody else, and longs for carpentry. These attitudes are no doubt supposed to make him extremely sympathetic to a modern audience. Supposing he had wanted to be thought cleverer than other people, and not to be exactly like them, it is clear that everyone's emotional sympathy with the idea that he should be given freedom to be himself would be decidedly lessened.

However, the play continues with Andri being told that he is like everyone's preconceived idea of a Jew until, when the revelation is made to him that he is not, he declares that he is. He has been treated like one for so long that he has come to feel like one. So you see we have the idea that the individual is completely malleable by social influences, and if he is treated as something long enough, will become it. This belief is, of course, exceedingly prevalent, and has the convenient corollary that if you treat geniuses as mediocrities for long enough, mediocrities is what they will become.

Containing as it does both this idea and the idea that what everyone most deeply wants is to be indistinguishable from everybody else, it is difficult to see what it has to do with its avowed theme.

The Ministry of Social Security

At the best of times I do not find human society a reassuring environment. But it came as a mild shock to the solar plexus to find that the 'Ministry of Pensions and National Insurance' had been renamed the 'Ministry of Social Security'.

The former was at least factual, and did not commit all and sundry to approval of pensions and national insurance (though the term 'insurance' verged on the tendentious.) But now we have an inbuilt evaluation of what the ministry is doing.

In no time at all the Ministry of Defence will be calling itself the Ministry of Peace or the Ministry of Brotherly Love.

I should never be very surprised if I found Kafka's Men waiting for me when I went down in the morning.

'In the name of the Ministry of Social Abundance,' they would say, 'we have come to take you away.'

And that would be that.

THE BASIC MORAL PRINCIPLE

IV: FREEDOM

24

The concept of property

The concept of property was one of the elements in the recent explosion in knowledge of the human race; later, perhaps, this quantum jump will be seen as an event comparable in effect with an ice age. At present, however, the aversion to acknowledging what happened is too great.

Proudhon, trying to assist the human race in recovering from the change in its affairs, observed, 'Property is theft'[3]. The concept of theft does not exist until there is a concept of property. All ownership implies that all persons other than the owner do not own the property. So you may say that ownership implies theft of what is owned from all who do not own.

Since life appeared on the earth, the use of all advantages has been bitterly contested. The right to enjoy the use of a territory or food supply has always been maintained by the ability to defend it against attack, even if it was not gained in the first place by attacking the former possessor. A rudimentary sense of possession perhaps arises in some forms of animal life. An individual may have his territory, his mate, his kill. These rights may

---

[3] 'Property is theft' (La propriété, c'est le vol!) is a slogan coined by Pierre-Joseph Proudhon in his book *What is Property?*

be to some extent respected by members of his own species but even within it are usually subject to being challenged by force.

Primitive human societies start to develop a rudimentary sense of individual ownership. Ownership is established in the first place by force, but it starts to be seen as convenient that individuals should not have to fight at all times to maintain, say, their huts and cattle, so the tribe starts to confer or to reinforce property rights. It can only do this, of course, within its own territory, and its ability to maintain the property rights of individuals within it will be lost if it is overwhelmed by some other tribe.

25

Property and respect for individual liberty

The principle of respect for individual liberty, to the extent it has ever been enunciated, is clearly not well-founded in the hereditary psychological tendencies of the human race. In its tribal past, individuals were expected to live out the life cycle as it prevailed in a particular tribe, with little scope for individual variation.

The concept of property, and the development of commerce, led to some respect for the individual in his own right and not merely as a tribal unit. If a person could pay for what he himself chose to have, then what he chose to have needed to be considered. And the idea of the individual as a numinous and slightly incalculable entity was vaguely reinforced by dualistic religion, which credited human beings with a spiritual component.

However, perhaps we should not be entirely surprised that the desire to subordinate individuals to social control, or indeed social oppression, should be a strong prevailing motive in human psychology. A strong tendency in modern intellectual life is the drive towards reductionism. Philosophers and psychologists will eagerly liken human beings to computers. Human individuality is entirely dependent on the physical; consciousness is something that arises when an evolving organic computer reaches a certain level of complexity.

This is all, in the main, very plausible. Throughout my life I have always supposed that any mental event had its neurological concomitants. However, this did not lead me to think that one should not try to obtain a life in which one could make use of one's intellectual and emotional resources, simply because one supposed that those resources had a physical substratum. Nor did it lead me to believe that the advice of social experts in my life should be sought and submitted to. (In practice I found such advice consistently to be very bad.) And I did not wish others to be forced to submit to social prescriptions and restrictions on their lives.

However plausible reductionism may be, the drive towards it has a motivation which goes beyond the desire for realism (not in itself a strong motive in human psychology). Reductionist theories are, it seems clear, seen as reducing the individual's claim to significance or autonomy, and as justifying social oppression.

Among the most favoured forms of research are those which add to the chemical control of the individual via his physiology, because these add in a practical way to the forces of social oppression; even if potentially useful to the individual, he cannot obtain free access to them as they are only available on terms of submission to the medical 'profession'.

It would seem that a willingness to submit to social oppression and a drive to have power over other people are very strong features of human psychology. There seems to be a positive drive towards social oppression of the individual, whether or not the person possessing that drive can play the role of an active oppressor (e.g. a doctor) himself, and even if he himself may be a victim of it. At the same time there is an easily evoked dislike of independence or ambition.

The drive towards an oppressive state of affairs in society goes hand-in-hand with the enjoyment of dishonesty in manipulating others. The average human being likes to make use of dishonesty, likes to see it being used by others, has little resistance to being taken in by it, especially when it is used by authorised social oppressors, and is resentful of others when they show signs of not being taken in by it. It is thus difficult almost to the point of impossibility to gain a hearing for any criticism of what is being done by social oppressors. There is bound to be a dishonest cover story of some kind, and if you should sound sceptical of its claims to be taken at face value you are likely to be accused of paranoia.

26

Free choice and slavery

It is interesting to consider how much of current 'morality', which may to a large extent be defined as the things people agree to be shocked at, is concerned with preserving the horizontal nature of society. There must be no hierarchies and no differentiation of function other than that prescribed by society. So we are shocked if a person behaves, and gets some other person to behave, as if there were such a hierarchy. We are pretty shocked at people who acquire some sort of moral ascendancy over other people so that they make decisions for them, even where this is a matter of free consent on both sides. Purveyors of various sorts of religion are a notable case in point. Perhaps they tell their followers whom they should marry! Perhaps they get them to clean the floors!

Clearly this does not arise from a great sensitivity about the issue of independent volition. Sensitivity about people being forced to accept decisions made 'in their own interests' by others is scarcely evinced in the case of socially accepted overlords – teachers, doctors, social workers and so on. And, indeed, in the case of religious gurus the issue hardly arises, as their influence is chosen by their followers. Then people are at pains to maintain that it is not a 'free' choice. Would-be religious followers are unfairly lured by smiles and friendship, which exercise an irresistible attraction for certain personality types. They are induced to sit through boring sermons, and to live in communal dwellings where they are underfed. Why do they stay if they don't like it? They are 'under pressure'.

Now, of course, if you are going to be so purist about it, there is no such thing as a 'free' choice. Society puts people under great pressure to think in certain ways and not in others. Parents and teachers lure children with smiles and friendship to accept their opinions, and at a much younger age than that of prospective religious converts.

One of the topics that there is much moral feeling about is slavery. And yet the choice of lifestyle, and ability to modify his own circumstances, open to a slave or serf has often been superior to that of people living in tribal circumstances or even in modern society. Chekhov's grandfather was a serf who bought his freedom. It is a great point, to be able to buy one's freedom.

Nowadays, there is no particular reason why one's education should open up to one the possibility of doing anything that one is suited to doing; there is no particular 'morality' in favour of releasing people from doing things which do not suit them in order to enable them to do things that do suit them. On the contrary, it is tacitly expected that anyone who finds themselves misplaced in the world will make light of their discomfort. 'Morality' is likely to be shocked by people who make unscheduled efforts to do things which society has not authorised for them.

However, if you *are* such a person, you soon realise how important it is to live in a capitalist society, in which there is at least a theoretical possibility (analogous to the possibility of saving up enough money to buy your freedom from serfdom) of achieving financial independence. This is not frequently mentioned as one of the great advantages of the capitalist system.

27

The 'protection' given by democracy

There is little point in pretending that any code of morality protecting human beings from oppression by one another has any secure foundation. Primitive human societies characteristically have little respect for human liberty or self-determination.

'Democracy' is a sacred word, and it is generally assumed that a 'democratic' society is automatically preserved from the worst kinds of social oppression.

In fact democracy, in the sense of everybody having a vote, protects one against very little in the way of social oppression. Even if each item of legislation were the subject of a direct referendum of public opinion, it is clear that one would have no protection against any measure which a majority of the people could be induced to believe was in their interests.

There is a tendency for what passes as morality, and the acceptable rights of man at the present time, to be regarded as in some way established or self-evident; probably this was also the case in societies which practised human sacrifice or slavery. However, democracy as we understand it, and the consequences to which it may lead, are relatively recent in the history of human civilisation.

When the American Constitution was drawn up, it was realised that a democratic voting system provided little protection for the interests of minorities, since it is self-evident that there is nothing to prevent 75% of the population from voting for a policy which will be very much to their advantage and very much to the disadvantage of the remaining 25%. For this reason a Bill of Rights was added to the American Constitution, which was supposed to safeguard minorities. But this only covered a few of the most obvious forms of oppression from which a minority might need to be protected.

The Bill of Rights did not, for example, insist that medication, medical information and medical procedures should always be available on a strictly free-market basis, whatever group arrangements people might like to enter into, or whatever group arrangements might be provided as a fail-safe by the state. No doubt in those days the medical 'profession' appeared less threatening and less offensive than it does now. At that time no doubt it appeared that obtaining medical attention and chemical resources was ultimately restricted only by financial means. The range of pharmaceuticals available was much more restricted than it is now, and it is only relatively recently that societies have acquired their present passion for making pharmaceuticals unavailable unless those requiring them should successfully lick a doctor's boots. And before the introduction of the NHS, situations seldom arose in which doctors were making decisions as to who 'should' receive the greatest amount of attention and resources on the grounds of their judgements about a person's likelihood of survival, and the 'value' of their life if they did.

Once a society conceives it as its purpose to do good to people, and not just to prevent them from doing harm to one another and to prevent society from doing harm to those who have not managed to remain self-sufficient within the rules, anything goes.

I used to suppose that there were a few moral rules that legislators respected, or knew they ought to respect. The first of these was that individuals should be allowed as much freedom as possible, so long as they did not interfere with other people's liberty. Secondly, laws should not be retrospective and should be as simple as possible; that is, they should depend on laws of contract. You should, for example, be able to decide whether you wished to be regarded as contractually married to another person, not subject to other people deciding whether the amount of time you spent together and the amount of money you spent on one another constituted a married state. That is, a person should, so far as possible, be able to plan his affairs with a definite knowledge of his legal position, not be uncertain how it would be assessed by other people.

And people who are in a normal state of competence should not be forced to enter into any relationship with another person in which they are not free to make decisions for themselves, i.e. the person consulted should remain a paid employee. It has never seemed to me offensive that persons should be other persons' paid servants; but that persons should be other persons' doctors, who are able to prescribe and to refuse chemicals, has always seemed to me abominable. However, I used to suppose that the immorality of this arrangement was recognised; that it was taken as a regretted, though mistaken, measure in view of the dangerousness of certain drugs. Now I realise that it is not recognised as immoral at all.

28

The welfare state and old people

The welfare state exists to eliminate freedom. Sometimes, however, even on its own terms, it is clear that a person 'needs' more freedom. For example, with increasing age a person's life, even if he is not particularly intellectual, deteriorates if he does not acquire a correspondingly increased amount of freedom with which to buy the services of other people. But rather than recognise this need as a need for increased freedom to purchase, the state forestalls recognition of the demand by making a very bad provision for the 'need'.

Nevertheless, ostensibly it is providing. An old person (to be happy) may need someone fairly constantly available to do small services and make preferred food and drinks at the times preferred by the person. But an old person is not given money to buy at least part of this service (it would then become obvious how much money was needed to buy what was really required). Instead a heavily cumbrous, not entirely inexpensive, but subsidised, Meals on Wheels service operates. Although pensioners pay, the aura is that of a charity. Access to the service is gained by an interview with an inquisitive person who asks the address of your doctor. There is no choice of menu, though the pensioner may indicate preferences to the organiser. You get what is provided on any given day; not every day of the week but four of them, so you have to remember which day it is and change your arrangements accordingly; and the food arrives at your door at the time convenient to the organisers. It is all a very effortful way of providing a poor substitute for a full-time domestic servant.

The only form in which extra freedom is conferred on an old person is in the form of an attendance allowance. This is extra money and, if he gets it, he can use it to pay anyone he likes to do anything he chooses – within the limits indicated by a maximum of about one-fifth of the average annual weekly wage. Age alone is no qualification; tiredness and frailty are not sufficient. When the examining doctor arrives to see if you qualify, by asking your next of kin insulting questions ('Is he ever violent? Does he get the right change when he goes shopping?'), he starts off by saying that there is no allowance for help you may need with shopping, cooking, washing or cleaning – in short, anything you really do need help with. No, it is only things in addition to that which count. Do you 'need' help with raising the food to your mouth? Dressing and undressing? (Undress now, please, to demonstrate your need.)

Now I wonder when an old person is deemed to 'need' help. How many hours must he struggle to do up his own buttons if his hands are anything short of completely paralysed. How many hours must he spend dragging his own bed linen to the laundry basket before he 'needs' help. No, we will only confer this precious bit of extra real freedom upon you, this extra bit of freedom of choice, if you can prove you are totally unable to do anything normal, if your freedom has been already so much diminished that we are quite certain this little bit of extra will still leave you well below the norm. Otherwise your needs are supposed to be provided for by the distasteful and inadequate state substitutes: the home helps who will come for a few hours (not when you summon them but when the state arranges), to do carefully chosen things (chosen by them, of course, as to what you may be allowed to need help with), while asking poky questions about your affairs; the Meals on Wheels. The state makes its gesture towards all the real needs of your life in these forms, and if you do not like them you cannot have cash as a substitute to buy at least a little help of your own choice.

29

Taxes to a landowner versus taxes to the state

In a film version of *Onegin*, based on Pushkin's novel, a girl in a landowning family says, 'It isn't right that one human being should be the property of another, just because of an accident of birth.'

It may not seem 'right', but there is nothing remarkable about it. I just happen to have been born in Britain, so I am the property of the British government, to whatever extent it sees fit to prescribe; and of recent decades it has seen fit to prescribe any number of restrictions on the rights of its citizens to make decisions about their own affairs, even within the most restricted territory.

It is frequently represented as oppressive that workers on the territory of a landowner were expected to pay him a tax of part of the crops which they produced for themselves. How is that more horrific than being forced to pay taxes to the government on practically anything that one earns or acquires in any way towards the improvement of one's position, and hence towards being able to do anything that one considers oneself to be worthwhile?

No doubt it will be objected that a tax paid to a landowner is only advantageous to an individual, or a small group of individuals, whereas one should be only too pleased to pay heavy taxes to the government, a large collective entity, which will distribute them in a way which a large collection of people considers to be 'beneficial' to an even larger population of people, i.e. the total population of the country as a minimum, and sometimes sections of the global population as well.

Actually, of the two, I would prefer to pay taxes to a landowner, because at least somebody would be getting something he wanted out of it. In the case of taxation paid to the government it is difficult to see whether the 'advantages' conferred on those members of the population who really want such advantages, and would pay for them with their own money if they had it, are not outweighed by the disadvantages conferred on other people (and sometimes the same people) against their will, because someone else considers it to be 'in their interests' to be disadvantaged in those ways.

I realise that I have this unusual preference because I like to think of people being able to get what they want to have, whereas most people only like the idea of people being prevented from having anything they want. As this is the majority view, it is bound to be the major determinant of what goes on in a democratic society.

It was when I was at Somerville that I first became aware of everyone's strange enthusiasm for having freedom (money) confiscated from people by taxation, and used to make distributions to other people by state agencies. 'But that will surely be very mechanical', I thought, 'and only very superficial considerations will be taken into account. Wouldn't people rather recognise the needs of those they happen to know well, into which they will have far more insight, and give their money to those people, rather than the government? I suppose as a fail-safe they could have a minimal automatic hand-out system, but surely the major burden of recognising real need will still fall on individuals.'

As it happened, I was myself about to provide a striking example of the inefficacy of state-administered 'benefits'. The hostility of the local education authority and of the local community generally, to which I had been exposed by the grammar school scholarship system, had ruined my education irrevocably, at least in the all-important essential of being able to derive from it a suitable paper qualification at the end of it, with which to proceed to a research scholarship and to an academic career. I had told many people at college about my problems, most of whom had not attended state schools, and some of whom could have afforded to give me financial help, even before they started to earn salaries of their own.

Whether or not my grievously anomalous position resulted from disadvantages consequent upon my relatively lowly social origins in comparison with theirs, I was clearly in desperate need of support in making efforts to remedy it. None of them provided it, then or at any time since, in spite of my continuing need for it, so I quickly realised that friendships formed at college are as meaningless as any others, when it comes to the crunch.

Gradually, also, I came to the realisation that their enthusiasm for 'aid' administered on a collective basis, rather than by individuals responding to the needs of other individuals of which they became aware, was an expression of their awareness that such aid would never result in anybody such as me, who knew very clearly what they wanted and needed it very badly, getting anything. State administered aid could be relied upon only to reduce people's freedom of action and their opportunities to work towards improving their position, never to increase them.

30

The transfer of freedom to agents of the collective

The welfare state, as some have called it, was the Trojan Horse which introduced a new hazard into human society. It might be the case that society was going to transfer freedom from those who had it to those who did not have it, but it was scarcely advertised that this would be done by transferring freedom to a large body of agents of the collective who would make decisions about other people's lives.

Taking a cross-section of people you know fairly well, do you really believe that they understand your needs in life so well that you would rather they decided what you should have than that you yourself should decide? Speaking for myself, I have found people to have the most inverted views concerning what was good for me, and I would not trust even people that I know quite well to produce a favourable result by any procedure other than consulting me carefully and taking care not to override my wishes.

However, the modern world has a peculiar belief that a good way of going on is to collect together a number of people to talk about a situation and do what they collectively consider most acceptable. The idea that this is a good thing may be said to derive from an impossibly idealised view of human nature. If people were profoundly rational, and good at communicating their views to one another, I suppose this might be a way of arriving at positive results. But in fact people are stupid, prejudiced and malicious, and human communication proceeds on a level of crude rationalisations. So all that one can expect to result from a committee-type situation is a decision that will reflect the generalised obtuseness and meanness of human psychology in a way that is compatible with the prevailing ideology. What we may be sure of is that no decision which is more generous or more enlightened than that dictated by the prevailing ideology will become accepted, because the majority of the people at the meeting will be strongly influenced by it, and all the meeting will really ensure is that nothing at variance with the prevailing ideology can possibly be done.

For example, when my mother was in an NHS hospital, they held a case conference at which many people who had anything to do with her (including myself) were present. In a very theoretical world this might have been an economical method of communicating information. What was in fact most obvious was the evasiveness in which Health Service professionals are doubtless trained, so that answers to questions consisted not of a detailed exposition of the facts, but of uninformative formulae designed to divert attention from the fact that the question was not being answered. Thus a question about whether my mother was getting enough calories a day was answered by the nurse with a statement that she was counting them and, under further pressure, that she would get a dietician to weigh my mother.

While one knows that evasiveness of this kind comes very naturally to human psychology, it does seem probable that all training courses for agents of the collective include specific instruction in the principles that go into this sort of thing. One wonders what the heading is: 'Communication skills' or 'Client care' or 'Self-assertiveness'. Anyway, it is clearly very difficult (impossible) to get out of an agent of the collective any information with which he has not been programmed to provide you, and you might save a good deal of fruitless effort if you were ever informed of what the 'guidelines' were.

* * *

When I criticise the state educational system or the NHS, many people hasten to assure me that it had done good things for themselves or their relatives. But I do not think that the state educational system or the NHS are acceptable either in principle or in practice, so here you have an illustration of the way that collectivism works. So long as a majority of the population is in favour of it, people can be forced to accept a system which they find totally unacceptable because enough other people are in favour of it. In a free-market system, however many customers profess themselves totally satisfied, you may still withhold your custom.

Respect for the autonomy of the individual is a recent ideal of the human race, even to the extent it has ever been an ideal at all. The history of recent centuries shows a fairly painful working towards a concept of individual liberty, and the greatest force in favour of the definition and defence of the individual's right to self-determination within a certain clearly defined area was the development of a commercial free-market society.

By the beginning of the twentieth century an individual was supposed to be fairly free to conduct his life without arbitrary torture or imprisonment so long as he did not break the laws; to hold his own possessions without having to defend them by force; to engage in legal transactions in which he sold goods or services in exchange for the wherewithal to buy goods or services himself. Those who had become rich enough to enjoy an appreciable amount of freedom defended it jealously, and this helped to define the importance of liberty even for those who had less of it. But freedom was very much a product of a commercial civilisation, and it would not appear that the human genetic constitution could have been highly selected either to appreciate and seek out freedom and independence for itself or to have much respect for the autonomous decision-making of others.

The principle of respect for human autonomy seems abstract, and relatively few people would find it appealing in its abstract form; nor indeed would they have clear-cut emotional reactions to its violation if the violation did not take a crudely obvious form, in which something obviously painful was done to them against their will.

Now as I see it, one of the cardinal principles of liberty is that a person should not be forced involuntarily into having decisions made about things which concern them by other people. This is not, in fact, what people choose to spend their own money on. Of course, if they wish to ask some expert to make a decision for them, that is a free choice on their part; but it does not force anyone else to accept subservience to that expert. This is what is so serious about modern collectivism; those who have the strongest possible objection to having decisions made about them by agents of the collective are nonetheless forced to accept this because a majority of people find it acceptable. And the fact that they do have a strong objection is not considered of any importance, because it is agents of the collective who decide which of the attitudes are to be judged as valid and worthy of consideration, and which are not.

To put this in concrete form, it is rather as if a tribe decides to shut everybody up in a small confined space for a couple of hours every day. Most people do not complain of this very much; but a few, perhaps those who have the strongest ideas of how they would wish to be spending that time, or who suffer from claustrophobia, do complain loudly and receive little sympathy from the majority. Should a person have a right to decide how important a given element of freedom is to them? A person who is buying an element of his freedom on free-market terms certainly will decide for themselves how important it is to them, as would be seen in our example if everyone could buy exemption from the daily periods of imprisonment by spending a certain amount of money.

31

Defence

There is a story about an Indian tribe which sallied forth to do battle with the American cavalry, protected by magical shirts which, as it transpired, were no match for real materialistic lead bullets. The accuracy of this story does not concern us now; it is only necessary to observe that what makes it appealing to the modern mind is the support it seems to give to the proposition that the modern mind has everything taped. People who were not modern had ridiculous superstitions about the way things worked, which were quite ineffective in controlling the environment. The modern mind believes in effective, prosaic things such as lead bullets and disinfectants.

However, on closer inspection it soon becomes clear that the modern mind has religious beliefs of its own about the way things ought to work and therefore must, and will, work. Any acid test which could seriously discredit these beliefs is thrust beyond the horizon of practical or foreseeable possibility.

For example, there are those who say it is merely wasteful to spend money on defending the country. One should not have to fight wars; the whole human race should live in peaceful brotherhood. (It is easier to believe in the brotherhood of the human race at large than it is to believe that a particular brother you happen to have would give you £1000 to bail you out if you were ever seriously in need of it.) And anyway, the argument continues, what is the point of fighting to prevent invasion? What would it matter if the Chinese were running the country? They would run it basically on the same principles we do. Everyone believes these days in human rights and social security. It would make very little difference. It is only old-fashioned chauvinists who think that nations differ from one another in gentleness and good manners.

This belief, or any other approximately similar belief, is only likely to be finally disproved when it is too late to do anything about it, in the same way that the Indians' belief in the supernatural properties of their tunics led them to expose themselves happily and confidently to a hail of lethal bullets.

32

Brief essays – IV

Communism and capitalism

Capitalism depends on certain aspects of the conditions in which we live – on the structure of time and the conservation of matter. The basis of capitalism is that if a tiger rushes towards you, you need a gun. If you acquired a gun at some point in time previous to the tiger's attack, and have it ready to hand, this is useful. If you have not actually got a gun, but know that you could acquire one at some point in the future, this is not so good. The problem is to survive so as to reach that future.

The essence of communism is that nobody may have guns unless everybody has guns, and the only way anybody can get guns is if the collective-at-large sees fit to make a universal issue. And you may not have a better gun than the collective sees fit to issue for everybody. So if the collective does not actually get round to issuing any guns at all, everybody will be equally liable to be eaten by tigers.

The Protestant work ethic

The Protestant work ethic is associated with the concept of capitalism and is supposed to advocate hard work and profit-making, self-denial and sobriety. Now whether or not these are to be regarded as good in themselves, hard work and self-denial had been required of tribal members since time immemorial. What distinguished the

Protestant work ethic, and lends some justice to its association with the rise of capitalism, was that it arose as one of the first attempts to make ethically justifiable that a person's efforts, and subordination of his immediate gratification, might improve *his own* position and lead to the furtherance of his own aims.

Private incomes

Let us suppose that in a population of 50 million there are 10 who are capable of advancing knowledge (this figure may seem excessive, but the principle of the following argument will hold good). If 1000 people out of the total population are granted a large private income, and this is allocated completely at random, there will be a probability of 1 in 5000 that one of the ten people who may do something will coincide with the possession of the means to do it.

If the possession of a large private income is not completely random, but is dependent upon membership of a property-owning class, this probability may be increased by a factor of up to 10, depending on how accessible to ability the property-owning class is. Ability is, at least to some extent, inheritable; and there is no doubt that the descendants of persons who have been able to become millionaires are more likely to have very high ability than the descendants of persons who have not.

This system is not, of course, perfect. It might only be the second generation which would have any chance to use its ability to function as intellectuals. However, nothing can be done about this unless you are prepared to arrange society so that persons of very high ability can become millionaires very early in life, say before ten, so that they can spend the rest of it being intellectual.

If, however, you have a society in which no persons out of the total population are permitted to possess private incomes, the chance of a private income coinciding with the possession of high ability will be exactly zero.

Feudalism

It is seldom remarked that mediaeval feudalism had its origins in socialism and was brought to an end by capitalism.

At the end of the Roman Empire, a welfare state prevailed, and the high level of taxation required to provide free sustenance for the unemployed population was ruining those productively engaged in farming. Small farmers, seeking protection from lethal taxation, decided to associate themselves with larger landowners, who were in a position to moderate the demands of the tax collectors by maintaining small private armies, thus enabling them to resist claims which they decided were unreasonable. This is how the mediaeval system originated in which peasants worked small pieces of land as vassals of an overlord.

One might see the analogue now in the unfavourable tax treatment of the self-employed and the great concessions which are allowed to highly paid employees of large companies; also perhaps in the favourable tax treatment of those who hand over their capital into the control of others, such as insurance companies, compared with those who retain control of it themselves as individual investors.

One may guess at the same psychological forces in both situations; maybe the late Romans as well as the late British hated the degree of individual autonomy which their Empires had unwittingly created.

Somerset Maugham

Schopenhauer observed that people don't think, but they have beliefs.

People don't notice what other people want, but they have beliefs about what they *ought* to want (and, even more precisely, ought not to want).

When W. Somerset Maugham was dying, he spent a lot of money on trying not to die until the last possible moment. Monkey gland extract for rejuvenation, people to wait on him, and so forth. This was what he wanted for himself; it was evidently the way he felt about the importance of his life to himself.

I have read a number of descriptions of his last days by people who knew him more or less well and visited him. Couched, of course, in tones of the utmost friendliness and benevolence, they unite in regretting that he was able to fulfil his own wishes. How much better it would have been for him, how much more appealing to all who had his *true* interests at heart, if he had been unable to afford all these remedies, and died quickly and gracefully. How sad it was to see him, frail and half-alive, eking out his pathetic existence.

I cannot recall that I have read any comment by a single friend of Somerset Maugham to the effect that it was a very good job he had the money to provide himself with those supports to the continuation of life which he clearly so intensely desired.

If he had not had the money, and if he had begged and pleaded with his friends to contribute toward the purchase of monkey gland extract – I wonder how many of them would have given anything?

Mother Theresa

I once saw Mother Theresa of Calcutta on my television set. It was a claustrophobic experience.

Like Somerset Maugham's friends, she too knew what everybody ought to want. I am always disappointed at the things that modern Catholics say. They used to say that people ought to want to do the will of God (which at least had the merit of total obscurity), or that there could be no solution to the world's problems until every single human being had accepted the authority of the Catholic Church, or that they couldn't possibly answer the question without getting their superior's permission.

Mother Theresa had no such scruples, and I cannot but feel that real old-fashioned vintage Catholicism might have thought her a bit presumptuous, in coming straight out with a recipe for putting everything right. Everybody ought to stop being greedy and love one another instead. 'How should they set about loving one another?' asked the interviewer. 'Smile at one another,' said Mother Theresa, dimpling. 'As simple as that?' said the interviewer, astonished. 'As simple as that,' said Mother Theresa, dimpling some more.

Then she went on to say that you ought to love people until it hurt. For a moment I hoped she might be about to say that if you loved them you quickly realised you could not possibly do enough for them, because you wanted them to have all they wanted; it would have been a bit of a relief to the claustrophobia if she had. But of course that wasn't what she was going on to say. She went on to say that there had been a crucifixion, and mothers suffered in giving birth, so it followed that love had to be painful. In this world, I know that counts as a rational response.

As for the smiling thing – people are pretty keen on smiling at you. It's a lot more common than giving you money, as I've noticed. After all, smiling is cheap, and even good exercise for the facial muscles. I remember, quite vividly, the way my teachers used to smile when they had me extra specially helpless.

'Trusting doctors'

In the description of a television programme about Dr Harold Shipman, the serial killer, the question occurred, 'if you can't trust a doctor, whom can you trust?' The answer is nobody, of course, least of all those who are given power by the state to interpret for you what is in your interests. (These least of all, because what is likely to attract people to such positions apart from the exercise of power over other people?)

Putting it the other way round, since nobody is to be trusted, how can it be considered reasonable to expect people to wish doctors and other agents of the collective to have power over their lives?

Carrie[4]

In the film *Carrie*, Laurence Olivier is the erstwhile respectable and well-to-do manager of a splendid restaurant who comes down in the world. When he is forced to take employment in a seedy café, where his standards of efficiency etc. are excessive, the manager takes obvious pleasure in dismissing him. This and other passages in the film appear to be inviting us to consider the proposition that people exploit and degrade those in positions of economic weakness. And, no doubt, we are also supposed to come to the usual conclusion that all will be well when everyone is in a position of economic weakness, every aspect of their lives being prescribed by agents of the collective.

'Psychological needs'

When people have attitudes at variance with modern ones, they are said to have a 'psychological need'. For example, someone might be said to have a psychological need to be critical of social experts or to believe in a hereditary elite.

But this ascription of psychological motivation is applied one-sidedly. I think you would have difficulty in finding contexts in which people were said to have a psychological need to believe in the welfare state.

Either side may protest that in wishing the highly paid to be taxed for the benefit of the less fortunate, or in believing that intellectual ability and many psychological

---

[4] This refers to the 1952 film starring Laurence Olivier and Jennifer Jones, not the 1976 horror film with the same title.

characteristics are inherited, they are only describing the state of affairs as realistically as possible. But it remains difficult to separate the process from 'psychological need' in any event, because if a desire to be as realistic as possible is in fact a person's only motive, what is it that provides his drive to be realistic rather than the reverse, if not some psychological need?

However, questions are less often asked about the psychological factors which may underlie ideas and attitudes which happen at the moment to be widely accepted, in fact invested with an aura of sanctity. Since the questions are seldom asked, there have been few attempts to answer them, and in attempting to guess what they may be, I proceed tentatively.

Government health warnings

Unit trusts are obliged to inform us that our investment in them can go down as well as up, slimming foods that they won't make us slim unless part of our calorie-controlled diet, and every packet of cigarettes must carry a Government Health Warning.

You could also have the following small message strewn liberally around the environment: 'Agents of the collective can do harm as well as good'.

V: EDUCATION

33

The evolution of education

There is a sense in which the authoritarian figures of a socialist society are far more authoritarian than those of a capitalist one. To illustrate this, let us consider the development of authority in the educational system, and the state of affairs regarded as acceptable at the present time.

In a primitive society there is no education in the modern sense. The child joins in activities designed to produce food and so on more or less as soon as he is able, and acquires practical skills from his elders as he goes along.

Education starts to arise when some individuals become rich enough to release their children in their early years from attending to physical necessities, and are either free enough themselves to teach them such things as languages and arithmetic, or can pay for someone to devote his time to doing so. So when teachers arise in the course of a developing civilisation they do so first as paid employees, or even slaves, of the parents.

As civilisation develops further, various charitable and communal efforts may be made to provide an education for at least some of those whose parents are not providing it for them, but this is clearly an imitation of what the parents who do provide for their children's education see fit to provide.

Finally it is recognised that the amount of effort people are prepared to make voluntarily to educate other people's children is incommensurate with people's ability to produce children to be educated; and the task of supplementing the private educational system is passed to the state, with its unlimited power to confiscate money from individuals.

This causes a great change in the status of the persons in roles of authority within the educational system. They are no longer the servants of the parents, they are agents of the collective, and they will feel free to assume a position of superior wisdom where parents are concerned, and even to interfere at will between parents and children.

The final stage in this process is not quite with us at the time of writing. The private educational system, shrunken by taxation and restrictive legislation as it is, is still present and provides a standard of comparison. By this standard it may be perceived that state schools may be very good at generating the right social attitudes and at interfering in people's lives, but private schools are still better at setting people up to succeed in life, with a higher standard of academic attainment and possibly certain psychological characteristics which result from a less degraded environment. It is therefore regarded as desirable that this standard of comparison should be eliminated altogether, and whatever is provided as education in state schools should be the only standard of what education can be.

34

Education and thinking for oneself

The socially correct interpretation of any situation may be arrived at by the application of a few simple rules. What is interesting is that the rules are never explicitly stated, but everyone arrives unerringly at the solution which the rules indicate. For the benefit of those not yet able to do this, here is a worked example.

Education is a way of enhancing natural inequalities.

There is no reason why the collective should wish people to learn to think. If analytical thought were something the human race cared for, rules for doing it could have been developed long ago. If these became part of the curriculum, there would have to be an end to party political broadcasts, and to most human intercourse for that matter.

The collective wants people to be good at absorbing propaganda. It wants them to accept unexamined assumptions, and to keep them unexamined. As a matter of fact, people are quite good at accepting propaganda, particularly if it is gratifying to their basic feelings of jealousy.

If anyone seems to be frustrated or dissatisfied with the education meted out to them, there is only one explanation. They must have had over-ambitious parents.

This follows because the agents of the collective are above criticism, so it cannot be that their teachers were jealous or malicious. Parents on the other hand are functioning as individuals so that all evil may be ascribed to them. The young person in question cannot really have been frustrated by society, because that is an impossible situation; society is the great source of all fulfilment. Therefore he or she was emotionally disturbed by over-ambition; but such an emotion as ambition can never be held to originate naturally in the young. Some evil individual must have influenced them, or it would never have arisen. The only convenient person to blame is a parent.

Naturally, it is held, if everyone is only brought up correctly by agents of the collective, or by individuals trained by the collective, everyone will want what society wants to give them.

If anyone should claim that their disagreements with their parents arose from the fact that their parents were not sufficiently ambitious on their behalf, they are clearly wrong. This is not possible; and, in any case no one will listen to them.

35

Children and Mill's principle of liberty

As quite a young child, I was under the impression that it was a basic principle of accepted morality and legislation that an individual's freedom of action should not be restricted except in so far as his actions might impinge upon the freedom of others. A century ago this principle was to a large extent respected. Provided you kept the law you could make your own decisions, subject to the resources and opportunities you had, and could try to enlarge your resources and opportunities. The law, it is true, violated the principle by including some moral elements, such as a prohibition of homosexuality, which could scarcely be justified as restraining the infringement of the liberty of others, as between consenting adults. A law of this kind was evidently based on psychological grounds, that people doing things of this kind might generate disapproval in others, and persons should be protected from having to feel such things.

Although the modern world has repealed the penalties for homosexuality between consenting adults, this is scarcely likely to have been out of concern for individual liberty; more likely the repeal was made because sex is the modern opium of the people, it being supposed that if they are encouraged to fill their lives with such harmless distractions they will not notice more serious oppressions.

Nowadays legislation is frequently justified on statistical grounds: that we must bring about a state of affairs in which society as a whole is the way we (that is, the legislators) would like it to be. I first noticed this when a law was brought in prohibiting the taking of what are now called GCSEs before a person's sixteenth birthday. Even at the time, and before I realised how serious the effects of this would be on my own educational prospects, I thought this to be surprisingly immoral legislation. Surely a person was not doing anyone else any harm by taking an exam younger than the average? The only harm you could be said to be doing was psychological: it might make other people jealous. But then the acquisition of any benefit in life might make other people jealous. If you started to take psychological considerations such as this into account you could plainly justify practically any restriction of individual freedom of action. What other people would like best would be to see you living a dull, unambitious life, enlivened only by such diversions as they permitted themselves, such as the aforementioned opium of the people.

Another way this sort of legislation is justified is by reference to protecting people from themselves. Thus in this case it may have been represented that children were being preserved from being made to work hard, or to 'cram', as previous legislation had preserved them from being made to climb up inside sooty chimneys in order to sweep them. This, however, leaves out of account all manner of individual differences, and does not allow the child or its parents the freedom to make a decision on the basis of his own abilities and temperament. The amount of effort that goes into preparing for exams is vastly different depending on aptitude and motivation.

Similarly, people are supposed to be preserved from choosing the wrong pharmaceuticals for themselves by being allowed to have only those which the doctor prescribes for them. They are not protected from the mistakes of the doctor, who cannot be supposed to have nearly the same interest in their wellbeing that they have themselves. Nor is the recipient allowed to use his own judgement to assess the likelihood that the doctor's prescription is more harmful than what he would choose for himself, in the light of the doctor's stupidity, incompetence, sadism, lack of interest, love of power, etc.

The principle that an individual should be free to make his own decisions, subject only to their not infringing in obvious ways on the freedom of others has, clearly, always been most vulnerable to abuse in situations of incapacity. There is an age before which an infant cannot make informed decisions for itself and must inevitably depend on its parents to make decisions on its behalf. In a similar way, a person suffering from physical illness may be genuinely incapable of making decisions for himself; in an extreme case, he may be unconscious. There may be no friends or relatives around. The fact that education and medicine deal, in their most limiting cases, with individuals who are not in any realistic sense able to decide things for themselves has, of course, led to extreme abuse. In both state education and medicine (even, though to a marginally lesser extent, in private medicine) there is supposed to be a complete transfer of concern for the 'interests' of the individual to a social authority.

36

Free education?

It is a long-standing truism that there is no such thing as a free lunch.[5] This is usually applied only in commercial contexts, where it is least applicable, because it is easy to see what people's commercial interests are and how likely they are to think they are serving them by providing you with a 'free' lunch. It is also true that there is no such thing as a 'free' education, 'free' medical attention, or 'free' any of the other things which a 'welfare' state undertakes to provide.

A 'free' education does not provide you with efficient training in academic subjects, for which you might yourself have chosen to pay (and would have been more likely to have the money with which to pay if a good deal of what might have been yours had not been removed by taxation in order to provide a 'free' education for everyone else). A 'free' education comes with a lot extra added in, because it comes provided with an army of people who wish to make value judgements about you and your children, and who want to make decisions of all kinds, for which they are not accountable to you, which are designed to have limitless effects on your children's outlook and attitudes in a large variety of ill-defined ways.

---

[5] This phrase was used in the 1970s by the economist Milton Friedman, as the title of a book, but was not originated by him.

A 'free' education is not the same thing as an education that you would choose to pay for, or your child would choose to pay for if the money to do so were directly placed in its own hands. You are not going to get what you want, or what your child wants, but what other people want to give you; and that, not surprisingly, provides them with a great deal of power over you and your child. So that although you may seem to be getting more than the simple provision of tuition, what you are receiving is actually much less; at least it will be perceived as much less by all those who wish to evaluate things for themselves, and who perceive the dangers inherent in the 'freely-provided' state of affairs.

It is one of the curious features of modern society that there is an effective taboo on recognising the possibility of negative motivation in agents of the collective. I once saw a quiz in a newspaper which was supposed to classify you as a 'hawk' if your answers indicated a tendency to try to get what you wanted by paying for it. One of the questions in the quiz was something on these lines:

If your child was not getting on at school and received a very bad report, would you (a) start looking through directories of private schools and select one with a good record where your child might get on better, or (b) ask for an interview at his/her school and have a frank and constructive interview with his/her teachers?

Certainly I would be very likely to settle for option (a), although I might try (b) first. But if I did try (b), it would be without the slightest expectation of its improving the situation. I would do it solely in the spirit of leaving no stone unturned before proceeding to the practical and realistic option of trying to get something worth having by paying for it.

On the basis of any discussion which my parents had about me during my education, I would expect the wildest unrealism to prevail in any such interview as that proposed by the quiz. I would always expect agents of the collective (i.e. in this case teachers) to be slippery and evasive, if not actively dishonest in the sense of making verifiably untrue assertions of fact. I would not think it likely that any conversation of this kind would illuminate the situation at all.

There is no particular reason why a school should provide an environment in which a given child can get on; there are many ways in which a school can generate demoralisation and discouragement, even if there are explicit exhortations to achievement. Psychology is a complex affair; in the course of my own education I formulated the principle that if the people running it were trying to arrange things in an advantageous way for me, they were very bad at doing this, and their understanding of psychology extremely crude, being based on a few fictitious principles. If, on the other hand, they were actually motivated to arrange things in a disadvantageous way for me, then they were very good at this, and their understanding of the psychological principles involved, although never verbally expressed, was amazingly subtle.

37

The unrealism of Herrnstein

Richard Herrnstein in *IQ in the Meritocracy*[6] suggests that in an era of universal state education, social eminence will be more closely correlated with IQ than it was previously. To arrive at this conclusion you have to make a number of assumptions which Herrnstein does not state explicitly and which are by no means unquestionable.

The first assumption is that a state educational system is IQ-neutral; it is an 'opportunity' equally applied; and we seem to be proceeding towards a situation in which no unequal opportunities, whether regarded as better, worse or just different, can be obtained by any means. Herrnstein seems to be suggesting that in the past the correlation of IQ with success was reduced by the fact that some children had a better education than others: some parents could pay for a private education, others could afford nothing better than that which the state system had to offer. When education is universal and identical (he implies) there will be no factors other than the individual's own attributes to make him emerge as more or less successful than others.

In the first place we may well doubt whether it is possible for an educational system to be neutral in its

---

[6] Richard Herrnstein, *IQ in the Meritocracy*, Little Brown, 1973.

effects on different levels of IQ and different personality types. It is in the nature of things that it will be optimally favourable towards certain kinds and levels of ability, and relatively disfavouring towards others. There may be no particular intention that this should be so, and it may be difficult to be certain what is being discriminated for and against, but there is no way of avoiding it. You would require a certain kind of personality and a certain array of specific abilities to be highly successful in the old-fashioned public school system, and it might well be supposed that a person who possessed them might not be particularly well adapted to succeed in a modern comprehensive school, which may well favour a quite different set of abilities and personality characteristics.

Apart from any other considerations, an educational system is almost certain to have a strong bias in favour of whatever is the prevailing ideology. In communist China, as I have heard, there are (or were) a band of prefects who supervise the ideological purity and correctness of the pupils' attitudes. Strangely enough, people constantly underestimate the strength of ideological bias in their own culture; but it would be naive to assume that because indoctrination with preferred attitudes is not explicitly labelled as 'Propaganda', nor even 'Right Thinking', in a modern comprehensive school, this means that no bias is present.

38

Child prodigies

Perhaps the human race is right to feel that the psychology of exceptional children (and even of any child that gets a chance to do something purposeful) should be so very carefully watched. There would seem to be a distinct risk of them getting into a favourable psychological position.

By the time you have provided yourself with an armoury of socially accepted myths (people with high IQs are often failures and it is all their own fault if they are / precocious children need to be made 'balanced' / child prodigies fizzle out 99% of the time / children who show signs of wanting to work have wickedly ambitious fathers / etc.) the way is open for full-scale psychological attack. Only the victim is going to get the blame if he cannot survive it.

Perhaps, when I was eleven and twelve, I managed to have the sort of advantageous psychology that they fear may arise. At any rate, I no sooner became aware of a psychological outlook with which I was strongly identified than it was opposed, and I was surrounded by references to child prodigies fizzling out. It took me some time to see the point, as I had never actually been allowed to do much.

But what actually I had, and what seemingly they found intolerable, was a strong internal sense of rightness and an infinite dedication thereto.

The first of my assailants was a nun; she was supposed to be teaching me maths but preferred to discuss how I could change. Nun though she was, she found my dedication intolerable. She described me quite accurately; it was quite clear that it was me being me that she disliked. I was, she said, not exactly obsessional, quite, but very single-minded. I couldn't exactly be called conceited, but I was dedicated to my exceptionality. I thought of nothing but getting on.

Apparently there was supposed to be some way of dislocating the central drive of your life and replacing it with a belief in society or human relationships. I couldn't see how it would be done and certainly had no intention of trying.

On the contrary, finding myself from this and other quarters so threatened, although without any clear idea of how the attack could become more serious, I made preparations for a future possibly dark. 'I shall never see things more clearly than this,' I said.

When the human race launched its major assaults on me it was assailing an unconditional resolution. That is not to say I survived undamaged; it was a psychological blood-bath. After all, the avowed intention was to dismantle my personality as it was. Once it was, in some way, broken down it would be more 'balanced'.

However abjectly unhappy I became, it was only taken as a proof of criminality and a justification for further treatment. That was quite right in a way, because the unhappiness was a sort of sign that I still hadn't broken in the required way.

As for the myth about child prodigies fizzling out; if many of them are subjected to anything similar, I'm not surprised. But in fact I think most are more easily deflected without such obvious head-on opposition.

Once you have lost contact with the central drive of your psychology it is not easy to regain it; this is a most difficult and little-known branch of psychology.

I have just thought of another amusing New Testament interpretation. There is that observation: Except ye become as little children, ye shall not enter into the kingdom of heaven.

One could try reading 'children' as 'single-minded child prodigies'. Very fanciful, of course.

But actually I did go to some trouble, during my first year at college, to reinstate the favourable features of my psychology as it had been at the age of twelve.

39

The distribution of IQ and its consequences

IQ operates on a normal distribution, that is to say, a bell-shaped curve with the great majority of the population fairly close to the mean and with remarkably high or low ability represented by tapering tails at the base of the bell. What this means, from a democratic point of view, is that it is very easy to secure majority approval for arrangements which are very unfavourable to the small minority with really high ability. If you can propose situations that are thought adequate by most of the population with IQs falling between 85 and 115, a massive majority is secure. The fact that arrangements are proposed which are extremely bad for a tiny minority falling within one of the tails will worry few people; in fact, on account of the presence of jealousy, this may even enhance their appeal to the enormous majority that lives under the dome of the bell.

This is, of course, equally true of the mentally handicapped, as they are now called, except that, as it happens, they are protected by majority acceptance of the ideal that people should be preserved from any ill effects arising from hereditary deficiencies. Indeed, I wonder if I am violating some principle of righteousness in referring to a lack of ability to deal effectively with the affairs of life as a deficiency. I think it is clear that at most times and places before the present century it would have been significantly disadvantageous to survival; the life of a village idiot or an incompetent swineherd was probably not a merry one.

So it is true that the lot of the people in the left-hand tail has improved tremendously, since everyone believes that now we are compassionate, and wishes good to be done to such people. This enthusiasm is probably all the greater because it is 'we' who decide what kind of good shall be done, the recipients of the benevolence not being in a very good position to define or express their real wishes. So they fit well into the dependent role which is found attractive in the objects of benevolence (even if it is at times decreed that they should learn to be independent in exciting matters such as making their own beds).

40

Egalitarianism

Although 'egalitarianism' is such a widely used and sacred word, its meaning, like that of many other quasi-religious concepts, is fairly blurry. It is much more difficult to justify if psychological factors are taken into account, so we do not do that. As a Japanese lady, perhaps in this context more outspoken than her British counterparts, once said to me, 'Intellectually precocious children have no right to special treatment.' They don't have a socially recognised right to it, or a socially recognised need for it, but they may have a need for it none the less. A person's needs are not identical with the needs that society recognises.

Modern society supposes that, in the person of the agents of the collective, it knows all about psychology. Again, what it actually does know is not too clearly stated (for fear that someone might start to disagree) but, as usual, whatever is actually taken into account, however blurrily, is supposed to be all that there is to know. Hence many psychological factors that a person might take into account in making plans for himself, or possibly for an offspring, do not have to be considered at all.

Even when egalitarianism has been reduced to a few crude and physical factors, it remains impossible actually to equalise people's life experiences. They will have different genetic endowments (until the medical profession starts cloning suitable types), they are brought up by different parents, even if those parents are members of the right age group to have been brought up in schools which purveyed much the same ideology. Even if they go to state schools and the conduct of their lives is under the influence of agents of the collective, even agents of the collective differ as individuals.

41

The socialist fallacy

There was in my father's view of human nature an inconsistency which might perhaps be regarded as the basic socialist fallacy.

When I was eleven or twelve I would sometimes see advertisements on the lines of 'Let me win the pools for you', or 'Subscribe to my infallible horse-racing tips', and I would say, 'Mightn't one at least try it?' But my father would say, 'What nonsense. If they really knew how to win anything they would keep the information to themselves, not sell it to you.'

I thought about this. I didn't see that it was entirely impossible that someone might have a generous motive. Perhaps they might feel that they preferred a steady, moderate income for themselves and would let other people have the chance of making more money in a more uncertain sort of way. My father's thesis evidently was that altruism and generosity were forces so feeble in human nature that you could rely on their not entering into any commercial situation even as partial motives.

But my father, I began to discover, was a great taker of advice. He would endeavour to implement the instructions of anyone with the smallest pretensions to a position of social authority, even if this meant a complete disregard for his own perceptions about the situation. He was prepared to believe that people who had never met me could tell him how he should treat me. 'But what does he suppose their motivation is?' I came to wonder. 'What incentive do they have to want me or him to be happy or successful?' It was true that they had no financial interest in ruining my life. They would be made no richer by my failure, any more than by my success. But that merely left it a completely open question what their motivation might be. If altruism and generosity were totally absent in commercial situations, we might surely suppose that these motives were not present in this uncommercial situation either.

42

Brief Essays – V

State education

State education is a contradiction in terms. The state represents the collective, and the collective wants people to be equal. It is easier to make people appear equally stupid than equally clever. If no one learns to read at all, it will never become manifest that some people would have learnt to read better than others. If no one is allowed to learn to read before the age of seven, it will not be evident that some people might have learnt to read when they were two, three, four, five or six. Of course not everyone will be able to learn when they are seven, so even this would only be an approximation to the ideal. Eight would be a better age, nine still better, and so on. The advantage of raising the age an extra year becomes smaller as one continues the process. The proportion of the population who can learn to read at eight, but not seven, is larger than that which can learn to read at nine, but not eight.

Nevertheless, any little bit of social justice is worth having. The ultimate in social justice in reading will be achieved when reading is made illegal at any age.

Quite apart from considerations of social justice, it is clear that the state cannot exactly want people to learn to think. It wants them to be good at assimilating propaganda.

Contrary Imaginations

Liam Hudson, in his book *Contrary Imaginations*,[7] points out that the conventional IQ test has failed to predict who will do outstanding work in science, and that there is likely to be no connection between adult IQ and adult achievement above a certain minimum which is about 120. A scientist with an adult IQ of 130 is as likely to win a Nobel Prize as one whose IQ is 180.

Apart from the possibility that IQ tests are not measuring anything which is operative or relevant in adult life, it may be pointed out that the success of scientists is also dependent on the situation within which they are working and the opportunities which it gives them. In the light of what actually goes on in most universities in the name of research, I find it quite easy to think that the way in which most scientists are expected to work does not provide scope for the exercise of any ability greater than that which is roughly correlated with an IQ of 120-130.

If you are given a task to do which requires a certain level of ability, the presence of higher ability is irrelevant. You cannot do more than score 100% in a probably fairly tedious operation. However, I would certainly suppose it was possible for research situations to be set up in such a way that not all persons with IQs of over 120, who were sufficiently well-informed and industrious, and not demotivated by boredom, were likely to do equally well at the research.

---

[7] Liam Hudson, *Contrary Imaginations*, Pelican, 1967, p.123.

Keynes and elitism

One gathers that Keynes is said to have been an 'elitist' because he thought the veneer of civilisation was awfully thin, so that you needed an 'elite' to protect it. (By which I suppose he meant an intellectual class permitted to have the conditions necessary to function as intellectuals.)

So far, in a rough sort of way, one might agree with him. It is easy to see the human race slipping back into barbarism, or into a sort of massive technological tribalism which one would find little better.

But Keynes's solution is 'equality of opportunity', i.e. selection of the elite by the collective within each generation. I suppose there must always be a temptation for those who, provided with the best private education and family connections, have arrived at positions of social recognition and salary, to think they would have done just the same from any start in life, and to credit the social forces that give them their present status with an infallible ability to select the right people, all the right people, and nothing but the right people.

Personally, not having a private education or any of the right family connections, I found the highest ability and the greatest determination insufficient to overcome the selective forces applied by my education.

Previously, it should be noted, the elite was not selected by a state educational system, but was self-selected. People criticise this process because some of the ways in which people rose in the world are not, in an obvious way, socially approvable. But it has to take genuine ability of some kind even to be a successful pirate or a king's mistress.

Private education and medicine

One advantage of paying for your own medicine, education, etc. is that you know what you are paying for, and you are somewhat less likely to get more than you bargained for.

If you pay for your child/dying wife/etc. to be in a private hospital, the chances are minimal that the hospital will incarcerate them on the grounds that it thinks you are not the right sort of person to look after them. In fact, a fairly simple method of regaining custody is to stop paying the fees.

Similarly with education. Although educators must always be under a strong temptation to think it is their business to understand psychology instead of teaching people things, you are not paying them to have your life run for you, your family relationships destroyed, your health and livelihood ruined, and so forth. One cannot say there is no risk at all of these things, since the tendency of human nature to do them for you is very strong, but again, you can always stop paying the fees and start again elsewhere. And, if you pay, you can start pretty fresh elsewhere; whereas if your child's education is under the control of the collective, changing to a new school would be sure to be accompanied by the passage of umpteen reports, which would ensure that you started off in just as bad a position in the new place.

Campaigns against Jews, aristocracy, etc.

I should like to make a parallel between the persecution of aristocrats in the French Revolution, the extermination of the Jews in Hitlerian Germany, and the hostility to ability and ambition, with the associated destructive attitudes to gifted children, in modern socialist Britain. In all cases the motive is hostility towards superior ability and the success that might go with it, and in all cases we see how completely unprincipled and destructive human nature can be, and fundamentally is, under whatever social conditions happen to prevail.

Good parents

In order to be a socially approved parent it is necessary not to 'push' your child. There is a social myth to the effect that great harm (of a quite unspecified kind) can be done by 'pushing' children. There is no corresponding myth about any harm that can be done by frustrating them; in fact, of course, 'frustrating' a child is not a possible concept. Even if it were ever admitted that a child had not been given opportunities for developing its abilities, this cannot possibly have done them any harm. This follows from the general principle that no social action towards an individual has any harmful consequences.

Benevolence

Once upon a time a headmistress said of me, 'It will be good for her not to be treated as an exception.' I found it very difficult to understand how she could even imagine that she honestly meant something by this, let alone something benevolent, since the sentence seemed to me to have the status of 'It will be good for this horse to be treated as a dog'. The use of the word 'good' in particular eluded me, until I reflected that there was in existence an expression 'The only good Injun is a dead Injun', and no doubt she meant something like that.

Willpower and work

It is supposed that:

achievement = ability x *willpower* x *time*

This leads to the supposition that if someone is given a great deal of time in which to do very little, and finds it impossible, they have, on this theory, the option of regarding either their ability or their willpower as deficient. In either case (if this is true) they are permanently incapacitated. But in fact the equation is quite different. It is more of this form:

achievement = ability x *incentive* x (*time* − *time*$_{optimal}$)

There are, however, cut-off points at which the form of the equation changes. If the level of achievement reached is high enough to set up a state of intensity, the equation becomes more like this, and *time*$_{optimal}$ has a lower value:

$$achievement = \frac{ability \times incentive}{time - time_{optimal}}$$

for *time* > *time*$_{optimal}$.

In other words, the level of achievement actually declines with time allowed above the optimal time.

If, on the other hand, the level of achievement declines below a certain level, the incentive factor drops to zero, because complete emotional inanition has been attained.

A Little Princess

A Little Princess by Francis Hodgson Burnett contains some psychological elements that are very antipathetic to the modern outlook. The little girl Sara reacts to adversity and ill-treatment by maintaining her own standards at any cost. However rudely she is spoken to, she continues to be scrupulously polite. This, of course, violates the modern rule about eliminating the tension between two alternative views of a situation by permitting only one; whether or not the modern rule actually arises primarily from the desire that the individual should have no right to claim that he is in any way different from the social view of him.

A modern contrast to the situation in *A Little Princess* occurred in the television prison series *Within these Walls*. The upper-class prisoner who started by trying to maintain her standards (in the crudest and silliest way, of course) was taken down a peg or two until she finished up discovering the demoralised delights of scrubbing floors in a resentful and disaffected way, calling the supervisors 'toffee-nosed bastards' (or something similar) as soon as they were out of earshot.

Actually I found this programme very interesting, the psychological atmosphere and techniques in the prison as portrayed being so reminiscent of a school I was once at. 'The court took the view,' said the wardress, with severe and carefully measured sympathy to the suitably drooping and unassertive working-class prisoner, 'that you murdered your baby under stress, and that you needed vitamins and help.' (So long as you do not expect anything more than society thinks you should have, so long as you accept that courts cannot possibly be wrong in their judgement of you, and so long as you remain dependent and have no positive view of yourself, you may have this small amount of sympathy that I am now giving you, some 'help' in the form of group therapy, and the vitamins.)

The cult of human relationships

The cult of human relationships, like any other dogma, becomes very dangerous when its sanctity is unquestionable. My education was ruined, and my father's health was consequently ruined, by people who claimed that human relationships were of overriding importance. The Spanish Inquisition was based on love, remember. It was run by people who knew so much better than the victims did what was good for them that it did not matter at all about overriding what they wanted. If you roast somebody at a slow fire you are giving them a lovely chance to repent of believing the wrong things; if you frustrate someone with a high IQ you are giving them a chance to turn into another sort of person.

Children as property

I see that in a case of some children who have been abducted and incarcerated by the state, on the suspicion that their father was giving them the wrong outlook, at least one journalist seems prepared to regard the fact that the lettuce fed to them in the children's prison made them sick as proof of the abnormal nature of their previous dietary habits.

There could be other explanations. Perhaps the lettuce provided in the prison was just horrible, or perhaps their digestions were upset by having been abducted and incarcerated. Or, more probably, both causes were operative simultaneously.

David Cooper in *The Death of the Family*, and probably a great many other similar writers, says the family is a bad thing because the children are regarded as the property of the parents. The point he does not make is that if they are not so regarded, they will be regarded instead as the property of the state.

EDUCATION

VI: CONCLUSION

43
Conclusion

I arrived on Earth via a multi-dimensional transit system and, as instructed, enquired the way to the nearest Bureau of Social Reassurance. I explained to the lady in charge that I came from another planet, and was very interested in the splendid way things were developing here. The scientists in my own world, I explained, had dimly got wind of developments by means of telepathy, but their information remained vague and they had sent me to make enquiries.

The lady passed me on to a psychiatrist, who enquired about my family relationships. I explained that in my world people hatched from eggs, and he referred me to a more senior psychiatrist. Finally, being convinced by my green skin, four eyes, and sundry other anatomical peculiarities, that I was actually not a native of their world, I was introduced into the presence of a very senior Social Adjuster.

'I'm delighted,' he said, 'that our colleagues in other worlds are taking an interest. We're always delighted to exchange ideas, and I'll tell you anything you want to know. But of course, you will be discreet about it, won't you? Say anything you like when you get back home of course, but it's not for publication on this planet ...'

'Well now,' he said, getting down to business. 'We have always had a quite remarkably difficult problem here.

There are two tremendous snags. The planet is much too easy to live on, and the human race – some of them – are much too intelligent.

'There are other kinds of animal that live on this planet, but the problem just doesn't arise. Take a cat, now. In its natural state it hunts for its living ... but even if you provide for it, it doesn't start writing symphonies, or inventing mathematics, or probing into things, or thinking about philosophy. It just sits and looks bored. Therefore it is quite safe to have it as a domestic pet and relieve it entirely of all material cares. It is frequently done, in fact.

'Of course,' the Social Adjuster said, rubbing his head, 'it may possibly be thinking about philosophy while it is sitting around looking bored. That's true of other animals as well. You can't be sure. But at least it never tells you if it does think. And it never tells other cats either. So the whole thing is perfectly all right,' he concluded brightly.

'But human beings are another matter altogether. Just where they got this unnecessary intelligence from no one quite knows. Some people think the ice ages had something to do with it. Life got a lot harder on this planet for a time, you know, and it may have placed an unfair premium on resourcefulness. But even that doesn't really seem to explain it. Other animals got through the ice ages without developing all sorts of superfluous interests, such as a taste for chess problems.'

In the playground, a crane was hoisting a very large wooden crate into the air, preparatory to setting it down on top of another large wooden crate. The children stood around in knots.

'This is a lesson in modern mathematics,' the Social Adjuster said. 'It is teaching the children that one and one make two. It makes it really practical and concrete for them. They make the cups of tea for the crane drivers. The class elects a representative to go out and buy the teabags.'

I decided I had learnt enough about Earth. 'It has been fascinating speaking with you,' I said. 'But I have just remembered that I left the gas on at home on my planet. Goodbye.'

Aphorisms

It is often suggested that if we thought too much about the 'negative' aspects of the situation (such as our death and finiteness) we should become depressed. Actually this is not the case; depression cannot coexist with the perception of existence. Even ordinary fear is readily distinguishable from depression.

* * *

On the whole Christian writers do not like talking about finiteness. They very much prefer 'guilt'. The sane person is particularly willing to believe that he is guilty of not being evasive enough. This leads to a cardinal value being ascribed to humility (cf. maturity – which it much resembles).

* * *

People treat Sartre like Quantum Mechanics; as if his *non sequiturs* were evidence of metaphysical profundity.

* * *

Wittgenstein was trying to prove that he was an automaton, but that nobody else was.

* * *

There is no need for such circumspection; the Kingdom of Heaven will not take you by storm.

* * *

When people talk disparagingly of rejection of the world (e.g. by mystics), they always make it sound as though the world were rich and full and juicy.

* * *

A piece of sane philosophy: Time *is* the succession of events.

* * *

'You mustn't confuse people by using these comprehensible analogies.'

* * *

There are very few ideas in any branch of science. The length of time which it takes to 'train' a scientist does not represent the time needed to learn to understand the relevant ideas. What takes the time is learning not to understand them.

* * *

All I ever do is to state the facts: sometimes they are so unfamiliar that it sounds as if I have made a joke.

* * *

The only way most people show evidence of a brain is in the cunning of their stupidity.

CONCLUSION

* * *

A short version of the New Testament

Thou shalt desire the knowledge of reality with thy whole heart, and thy whole mind, and thy whole soul, and nothing whatsoever beside it.

Blessed are they who cry for the moon, for they shall inherit the sun.

To him that shall wake in life and know it to be a dream, all power shall be given in heaven and in earth.

* * *

A sane person will rarely admit that there might be alternative states to that of sanity. But if he does, he will make the alternative sound ludicrously easy, and he may go on to justify it by sane criteria. People writing about mysticism are very similar to existentialists in this respect. ('Of course not everyone is cut out for communion with God, and I think you have to be careful that it isn't escapism, but if you're quite sure that it isn't leading to any loss of contact with life then I think it may be a good thing, and I have known a few people who were decidedly the better for their mystical experiences and became very active in welfare work.')

* * *

I must draw your attention to a new form of reification which has become fashionable. The old kind took abstract notions seriously and identified them with invisible entities. (E.g. The All; the Spirit of the Age.) The modern version is used to deny that abstract notions make any sense, and consists of identifying them with visible concrete objects. E.g. Time *is* the succession of events; Christianity *is* hundreds of millions of persons.

* * *

Whatever I am and am not
Whatever I possess and do not possess
Wherever I am and however I came here;
I devote all that I am and possess, such as it is
To the purpose of research into the nature of the universe
From now until my death,
Or the changing of the world.[8]

'Because I believe that I know what I am,
And because I think that what other people tell me is right,
I will do as many things as possible that other people have always done
And I will not think about the universe,
Because I can always pretend that I shall never die.'

* * *

Mysticism is about modifications of consciousness. It is generally assumed that the modifications produced are of a sleepy, unrealistic variety; towards an undifferentiated calm; a vegetative merging with the subconscious; perhaps a return to the prenatal state. The best kind of mysticism is supposed to be that which is associated with great activity in the building of hospitals.

---

[8] This is a formula I made up for myself when I was about seventeen.

CONCLUSION

* * *

On writings about human psychology

We have to bear in mind that descriptions of human psychology and social arrangements are made by people who are themselves members of human society; hence many of the most salient features of human society pass without comment.

* * *

The belief in society

Now it is clear that before any change in human psychology, either individual or collective, could take place, it would be necessary for the belief in the meaningfulness of human society to be abandoned. (The resistance to its abandonment is of course immense.) It is true that this is only one of the attitudes which is invalidated by the perception of total uncertainty: but psychologically it is the lynch-pin of the whole affair. If you *never* believe that human society, or collective opinion, can confer any meaningfulness upon your actions or attitudes, you can never develop the human psychosis in a permanent form.

* * *

Individualism

It is difficult even to use the term 'individual' or 'individualism' without invoking a set of implications which one may or may not intend. Current 'morality' and 'idealism' (it is not called by either of these names, but is what people rely on for justification of indignation) is largely anti-individualistic, if the matter is viewed in a certain way. 'Individuals' have a 'right' not to be 'dominated' by other individuals. Their rights are to be protected against one another, not against collective influences.

* * *

Their religions are full of guilt and forgiveness. If the situation were really about this, ignorance of the rules might indeed be an excuse. But in fact it is much more that if you stand in the path of an avalanche it will kill you, and it will not be interested in how well you pretend not to see it on the way. (This is a bad analogy because it sounds as though only a narrow strip of terrain was threatened; whereas in fact only a narrow strip is safe.)

* * *

The truth is very far-fetched.

About Oxford Forum

Oxford Forum is a research organisation which was set up to oppose increasing ideological bias in mainstream academia. Its aim is to expand into an independent college cum university which would generate and publish research in several areas including philosophy, economics, the psychology and physiology of perception, and theoretical physics.

Oxford Forum is seeking potential patrons to provide funding for its activities. We are also looking for additional associates to help with our expansion plans. Further details and information can be found at www.celiagreen.com and at oxford-forum.org.

An appeal for funding

There appears to be an underlying belief in the modern world that if you are not in some socially recognised position or category, you cannot be deserving of any help, especially money, to get into a different position or category; and even if you fit into some category, no individual should consider it their business to help you, because you should be able to get help from some recognised source of funding for the social category into which you fit. I have to say very explicitly that I do not accept this belief.

I am appealing to any individual, who considers himself tolerably provided for, to recognise the fact that I am not, and that I am only being prevented from contributing to the intellectual life of my time by lack of salary or financial support.

I am also hereby making a direct appeal for financial support to any institution which is able to provide it, as well as to any university or source of funding for universities.

Despite appearances we (I and my associates) are an independent university — with an associated publishing company — prevented from appearing as such by a severe lack of funding. We aim to maintain the academic standards which modern 'universities' have allowed to deteriorate, as their primary purpose has become the support and promotion of a particular ideology.

Oxford Forum is underfunded and understaffed, although my colleagues and I are attempting to support it by means of entrepreneurial activities. The smallness of our scale of operation at present is caused only by the lack of both money and manpower, which we are attempting to overcome as fast as resources permit. We are entirely self-supporting, which severely curtails our activities.

I am also hereby appealing for people who are prepared to act as genuine supporters in presenting our need of support to other people who might be able to provide it. There is not the slightest use in our making applications on our own behalf without such support. This I have concluded as a result of extensive experience, and my conclusion was confirmed by a fund-raising specialist whom we consulted.

Celia Green
Director, Oxford Forum

Some other books published
by Oxford Forum are described
on the following pages.

For further information please visit
www.celiagreen.com

The Human Evasion

Celia Green

'On the face of it, there is something rather strange about human psychology. Human beings live in a state of mind called 'sanity' on a small planet in space. They are not quite sure whether the space around them is infinite or not (either way it is unthinkable). If they think about time, they find it is inconceivable that it had a beginning. It is also inconceivable that it did not have a beginning. Thoughts of this kind are not disturbing to 'sanity', which is obviously a remarkable phenomenon.'

The Human Evasion is an attack on modern thought, revealing the patterns of prejudice which underlie its most cherished opinions. Surveying the whole field of modern thought, the author reveals the same disease at work in modern Christianity as in theoretical physics.

'Anyone who reads this book must be prepared to be profoundly disturbed, and in fact looking-glassed ... Few books, short or long, arc great ones; this book is short and among those few.'
R.H. Ward

'Refreshing ... so much sparkle.'
The Observer

ISBN 0 978 09536772 45

Advice to Clever Children

Celia Green

'Young people wonder how the adult world can be so boring. The secret is that it is not boring to adults because they have learnt to enjoy simple things like covert malice at one another's expense.'

Celia Green provides a personal guide to the pitfalls and polite fictions which may await the gifted child in the adult world. With the author's usual lucidity and astringent humour, this subtle and provocative book develops the powerful ideas first outlined in *The Human Evasion*.

'Celia Green has written an important and mentally stimulating book which goes far beyond its title. Herself a brilliantly precocious child, she details some of the difficulties such children go through. She goes on to set out and reflect on her philosophy of life and displays some strikingly original ideas. This is a book which will repay careful reading and study.'

Lord St. John of Fawsley

ISBN 978 09536772 21

The Abolition of Genius

Charles McCreery

An analysis of the relationship between genius and money. Charles McCreery puts forward the controversial thesis that the possession of a private income, either by the genius or by his or her patron, has been a necessary condition of the productivity of the great majority of geniuses throughout history. His analysis is illustrated with many examples. He exposes the myth of Mozart's poverty, and shows how many of the great English poets, including Keats, were the beneficiaries of a private income.

Dr. McCreery discusses why financial independence is likely be a favourable status for geniuses, and explores the psychological effects of being dependent, or not, on the goodwill of others. His analysis raises the question of whether modern collective entities, such as the Arts Council, can effectively replace the individual wealthy patron of the past.

'This is a courageous, well-argued and timely book.'
Professor H.J. Eysenck

ISBN 978 19160906 13

The Power of Life or Death

Medical Coercion and the Euthanasia Debate

Fabian Tassano

'The assumption that medical professionals always act benevolently has been used to justify giving them increasing control over their patients. Like any power, this control can be abused ...'

A shocking analysis of the reality behind the image of doctor-patient trust, and an incisive examination of the claim that patient autonomy has increased.

'A terse, clear, incisive, intellectually first-class study of the growing power of doctors and of the lack of effective checks upon the surely numerous abuses of that power.'
Professor Antony Flew

'Tassano presents hair-raising case studies ... his book is a timely polemic.'
Literary Review

'His view goes straight to the medical jugular.'
Nature

ISBN 978 09536772 07